P

Think This Not That

"Rita Schulte understands how tough life can be. In 2013, her husband of nearly thirty-seven years took his life. As a psychotherapist and trauma survivor, she knows suffering can often make us lose heart and become confused about our lives. Left unchecked, negative thinking can even lead to illness. In this book, Rita explores current research on neuroplasticity, which has proven that we can change toxic thinking patterns into positive ones, and she provides the practical tools you need to eliminate toxic thinking for good."

—Dr. Tim Clinton, president, American Association of Christian Counselors

"If you're serious about changing how you think and are ready to devote the time to do so, you need to read this book. As a clinician and trauma survivor, Rita knows what it takes to turn the most difficult story into something redemptive. Follow her on her journey and find freedom!"

—Jennifer Cisney Ellers, counselor, life coach, and trainer,
Institute for Compassionate Care

"Often we pick a book because of its content. And don't get me wrong, the content of this book is as solid as it comes. Not only does Rita describe how our brains are wired but she does so with the grace and compassion of one who sees every day from her counseling office how our 'stinking thinking' holds us back from being truly alive. This book is full of helpful ways to start changing how you think today. But, the most important reason you should pick up this book is because Rita lives her message. I have watched her walk through unbearable pain, yet she continues to live fully alive because she applies these principles. This is an author you can trust."

—Joshua Straub, PhD, author of *Safe House: How Emotional Safety is the Key to Raising Kids Who Live, Love, and Lead Well*

5/27/24

neural circuits
nureons connected
by synapses to carry
out a function when
activated
chemical syn— allew
neurons to form circuits

THINK THIS
NOT THAT

THINK THIS
NOT THAT

Rewiring

Your Brain

to Eliminate

Toxic Thinking

RITA A. SCHULTE, LPC

LEAFWOOD
PUBLISHERS
an imprint of Abilene Christian University Press

THINK THIS NOT THAT

Rewiring Your Brain to Eliminate Toxic Thinking

LEAFWOOD
P U B L I S H E R S
an imprint of Abilene Christian University Press

Copyright © 2018 by Rita A. Schulte

ISBN 978-0-89112-579-2 | LCCN 2017048781

Printed in Canada

Published in association with the Hartline Literary Agency, 123 Queenston Drive, Pittsburgh, PA 15235.

Library of Congress Cataloging-in-Publication Data
Names: Schulte, Rita, 1954- author.
Title: Think this not that : rewiring your brain to eliminate toxic thinking
    / Rita A. Schulte, LPC.
Description: Abilene, Texas : Leafwood Publishers, 2018.
Identifiers: LCCN 2017048781 | ISBN 9780891125792 (pbk.)
Subjects: LCSH: Thought and thinking—Religious aspects—Christianity.
Classification: LCC BV4598.4 .S38 2018 | DDC 153.4/2—dc23
LC record available at https://lccn.loc.gov/ 2017048781

Cover design by ThinkPen Design
Interior text design by Sandy Armstrong, Armstrong Design

Leafwood Publishers is an imprint of Abilene Christian University Press
ACU Box 29138
Abilene, Texas 79699

1-877-816-4455 | www.leafwoodpublishers.com

18 19 20 21 22 23 / 7 6 5 4 3 2 1

Contents

ACKNOWLEDGMENTS

There are many to thank along this long and difficult journey that led to the writing of this book. Many walked alongside me and helped me guard my own toxic thoughts and refute the lies that the enemy of my soul wanted to use to dismantle my struggling faith, to destroy my belief in a good and loving God, and thereby to render me useless for his kingdom work. With the help of these dear souls, I am emerging from the dark abyss of grief and despair, and I pray that this book will be a resource of sound instruction and biblical hope. To Ashley and Michael, my beloved children, and to my friends, Patty, Shanda, Donna, Debbie, Ann, Gail, Caroline, my sister-in-law Tori, Jennifer, Honor and Heather, and my brother-in-law Grant. I am eternally grateful for your love and support.

I would like to thank my dear friend and personal assistant Patty Jo Diamond for her invaluable help with this project, as well as the idea for the title. Her constant stream of ideas keeps me on my toes, inspires me, and keeps me laughing constantly. To all those who have walked through a dark night of the soul where toxic thinking has threatened to overtake your very soul, I pray that this book will offer hope, not only scientifically, but most importantly, that it will connect you to the heart of the healer, our Lord and Savior Jesus Christ.

INTRODUCTION

Fear. Anxiety. Depression. Suicidal thoughts. Hopelessness. These are hard words to write, because behind them are the hundreds of sad and heartbreaking stories I've listened to during my years as a psychotherapist. These words reveal the hearts and souls of real people struggling with real-life crises.

This project has been rumbling around in my mind for the past few years for several reasons. As a clinician, I have seen how destructive thought-patterns have dismantled the hearts and lives of so many of my clients, causing them to hide, causing them to feel shame, causing them to believe they were unlovable, no-good, inadequate—that they would never measure up. I've seen them withdraw, isolate, self-harm, become addicted to something, and shut down their hearts. I've been privy to how the lies they've believed about themselves, about God, and about the world around them have kept them from doing the one thing necessary for healing—telling their stories.

But today I have an even deeper purpose and motivation for this work because I have witnessed and experienced the power that lie-based, toxic thinking can have in a heart and mind already wounded. These thoughts and lies can bring condemnation, shame, destruction, sickness, and death. I have seen how such deception can overtake a sick mind and make it sicker, how it isolates and destroys God's creation. I saw it kill, steal, and destroy my husband of thirty-eight years, causing him to end his life.

I'm talking about everyday people like you and me. Some get better—others don't. As a counselor, a piece of my heart always goes with them. I am saddened by the losses that have left indelible scars on their souls. As I've sat with people of all ages throughout the years, I have seen the same themes and patterns that led to the breaking of my own heart. I've seen deception.

Their stories, as well as my own, are the catalyst that led me to write this book. They demonstrate one bedrock truth: *What we tell ourselves determines everything in our lives, because what we tell ourselves is a direct link to what we believe about everything.* Our beliefs about self, God, and the world around us drive our behavior both for good and for bad. In this book, we'll take a look at how deceptive thinking begins, the problems it causes in our lives, the factors that keep it in play, and most importantly, what we can do to achieve real and lasting change.

The book is divided into three sections. In Part One, using the lens of attachment theory, we'll look at how deceptive messages are encoded in the brain. We'll look at how the distractions of the world can contribute to deceptive thinking. We'll have a short lesson on brain neurobiology to learn how the mind is different than the brain and how, by harnessing the power of conscious awareness, the mind can make choices to change the architecture of the brain. We'll see how buying into deception fuels the fire for dysfunctional belief systems to grow and thrive. We'll see how our neuro-networks are wired through the process of Hebb's Law, as well as the exciting role neuroplasticity plays in rewiring the brain's neuro-networks.

In Part Two, we'll look at research by Karen Reivich and Andrew Shatté and see how our explanatory styles impact our minds and keep us stuck in negative thought patterns. We'll learn about the eight major cognitive distortions and how they feed deceptive thinking. We'll learn about how set-in-stone beliefs drive our behavior. We'll look at cutting-edge research on shame, using the lens of Brené Brown's work. We'll take a look at how shame affects us and learn what we can do about it. I'll walk you through the story of my husband's suicide and the ensuing Post Traumatic Stress Disorder I developed, and then I'll show you how I found freedom by using the techniques outlined in this book.

In Part Three, we'll look together at how to build new memory bases by replacing deception with truth, how specific calming and focusing exercises can and will change your brain when they are practiced with intentionality, and how learning the power of reflection and writing can integrate right-brain and left-brain hemispheres. I'll educate you on how practicing presence can lead you back to be your authentic self. Most importantly, I'll share with you how God showed up in my life when I learned how to practice *his* presence through the use of the spiritual disciplines, all of which change the dynamics of the brain.

As we get ready to dive into this life-changing study, here are a few key points we'll be addressing in this book:

- Your mind is the most powerful God-given part of you.
- Your mind is *not* your brain.

- Your thoughts are vitally important. They drive your belief systems and *your actions always follow your beliefs*.
- If you change your thoughts, you can change your life (your behavioral responses to life circumstances).
- You can learn to *notice* your dysfunctional thought patterns.
- You can learn how cognitive distortions are keeping you stuck.
- You will understand how Hebb's Law, which says neurons that fire together wire together, impacts your habits and the ways you process them.
- You can learn how to lower anxiety and stop ruminating.
- You can train your mind to choose wisely (1 Cor. 2:16b).
- You can calm your mind and body through the focusing exercises that will be provided.
- You can renew your mind (Rom. 12:2) because you can learn how to focus on truth and thus create new neuropathways in your brain.
- You can learn the power to direct your mental attention and, in the process, shape your brain's firing patterns.
- You can develop your inner life through intentionally practicing the presence of God.
- You can choose your responses to the events of your life—even when it feels like the bottom has dropped out of your world.
- Since your brain is designed to have neuroplasticity, it can be rewired.
- You can overcome feelings of bitterness and rejection.
- You will learn techniques that will help integrate your right and left brain for a healthier and more balanced emotional life.

- You will learn how to enter into deeper connection with God.

If you feel like you're stuck in the same old rut of ruminating about things, worrying, fretting, feeling anxious, and being just plain miserable about your life, now is the time to equip yourself by learning how the power of your thoughts is affecting you. If you can learn to train your brain to think on *This* (what is pure, noble, pure—Philippians 4), then in time, you'll like the way this feels so much that you won't want to think on *That* (negative, self-defeating thoughts). So join me on this magical mystery tour of the most amazing organ God created—Your Brain!

PART ONE

HARDWIRED
AND HOOKED

WHAT'S DOWNLOADING ON YOUR HOME SCREEN?

Turn my eyes away from worthless things.

—Psalm 119:37

Men are not prisoners of fate, but only prisoners of their own minds.

—Franklin D. Roosevelt

Deception. It can be subtle. We hear something. We think something. We internalize something. We are *unware* on a conscious level how it affects and misdirects our thinking. Deceptive thoughts take root in the mind, and the connections made through the habitual process of ruminating on toxic thoughts form powerful neuropathways that literally shape our brain. The good news is that we have the power to change all this. With all we've learned about brain science over the past two decades, we now know that we can change the physical nature of our brain by consciously directing our thoughts to what is good (Phil. 4:8).

How? By learning to pay attention. It all begins in the mind, and it all hinges on what we think. We get to choose what we set our minds on, and as we consciously direct and focus our thoughts to what is good, we can learn to think on *This* (truth) and not *That* (negative thoughts) while changing the architecture of our brain. How is this possible?

First, through neuroplasticity, the brain's ability to reorganize itself by forming new neural connections (more on this later). Second, through "neurogenesis," the growth of new brain cells. Researchers have discovered that each of our brains contains a population of neural stem cells that are continually replenished and that can differentiate into brain neurons. Simply stated, we are all experiencing brain stem cell therapy every moment of our lives.

What does this mean for us? It means that we have the power to fight against toxic thoughts that keep us stuck in negative thinking patterns. It means we can ameliorate the negative neuropathways and wire in new ones by appropriating new ways to think and live. In this book, I hope to show you just how critical focused attention will be to changing your thought-life and your brain, and how, by using the techniques outlined here, you can improve your mental, spiritual, and emotional well-being. It all begins with self-awareness.

The Cause and Effect of Deception

If you aren't convinced about the power deception can have over your thought-life, think for a minute about how a magician fools you. Through sleight-of-hand (manipulating your ability to focus), he misdirects your attention so that you have no chance to focus on what is actually occurring. Take master-pickpocket artist Apollo Robbins, for example. He can steal just about anything from you right on the spot without your even realizing he's doing it! How? Simple, he manipulates your ability to stay focused. You can see how he does this by going to Youtube and searching his name. There are several really fun clips to watch.

Apollo is able to steal people blind because they are distracted and, therefore, unaware. If you're like me, as you watched some of Apollo's videos, you probably didn't notice all the things that were going on. The same thing is true with our thought-life. Think for a moment about everything in your life that's keeping you distracted, even when you're trying to stay focused. Your mind wanders to your kids, your work, your family, problems with relationships, worrying about your body image, your finances, your unmet needs, your losses. It's overwhelming!

Most of the time, we aren't paying close attention to what we're paying attention to, so we don't realize the distractions, or how our negative thinking patterns are affecting our mood, health, belief systems, and our brain moment by moment. All this information has a powerful effect on the mind, and while you are thinking, your brain is busy making proteins that form the thoughts that lay out the landscape of your brain—for better or worse.

While you may never have to worry about a master-pickpocket deceiving you, there are other forces even greater out there that you do have to be concerned about—forces that are influencing your mind on a daily basis. We'll look at some of them in this chapter, and hopefully you'll be able to determine if some of them are contributing to any negative thinking in your own life.

The first is Satan, the Enemy of your soul. He is out to kill, steal, and destroy. While he condemns, accuses, and distracts, his number one tactic is to deceive. Take a look at 2 Corinthians 11:3, "I am afraid that just as Eve *was deceived* by the serpent's cunning, your minds may somehow be *led astray* from your sincere and pure devotion to Christ" (italics mine).

What are the effects of being "led astray"? Distraction and a roaming from the truth. Satan's goal is to push you into making a commitment to believe the deception. Once you breathe the lie into your soul and believe it, he's got you. Why? Because your

your

actions will always follow your beliefs! You will live and act out of whatever you chose to believe, and you'll hear me say this over and over throughout this book.

What does deception look like in today's culture, and how does it wreak havoc on the human soul? Drug addiction, alcoholism, pornography, marital infidelity, eating disorders, anxiety, and depressive disorders—to name a few. How does it happen? Let's take a look.

A Few Clicks Away

David came into my office because he was having marital problems. His wife caught him using pornography and issued an ultimatum: get help, or get lost. Dave had a high-stress job with lots of people depending on him, but he liked the feeling of being needed. His home-life was even more stressful. His wife was demanding, and he had four kids. He told me his wife wasn't very interested in sex after their last child was born, and he was really struggling with it. All the stress in his life was killing him, and there seemed to be no release.

He said the porn thing started out of curiosity when he'd get pop-ups online. One day he made the one fatal click that started things rolling. Dave found that watching pornography relieved his stress, and before he knew it, he was hooked. It got to the point where he was craving his time in front of the computer every day.

PORN Looking at pornography relaxed him. It was a mindless task that took him away from his stress. Unfortunately, his continued use reinforced the behavior (feeding the pleasure centers in his brain) and hardwired the behavior into his neuro-networks, teaching him that whenever things were stressful or he felt devalued by his wife, he could relieve the uncomfortable feelings he experienced by disconnecting and looking at porn.

22

David was totally unaware of how something he started out doing only occasionally eventually took over his thought-life. How did David, or, how do any of us, get ourselves into these mal-adaptive ways of coping? It happens because (a) we aren't paying attention to what we're paying attention to, (b) we are misdirected into thinking that happiness lies "over there" (as my friend Patty says), and (c) we are deceived into thinking that if we just had _____ (fill in the blank), we would be happy.

Think about it, the women I counsel who have eating disorders don't over-exercise, starve themselves, or binge and purge because they like it. They do it because they have been deceived (by peers, media, TV, Internet) into believing that if they weigh *this* (mind you, nothing is ever good enough), they will have *that* (value/worth, adequacy, happiness, someone to love them).

David started looking at pornography because it relieved stress and met some needs for him (sexual gratification and feeling adequate as a man). His beliefs about his situation and his rationalizations led to a full-blown addiction. The same process is true for whatever maladaptive patterns we develop, whether it be alcohol, gambling, sex, shopping, or being a workaholic.

It can even be something as simple as avoiding stressful situations, people, or events where you have to face conflict. If conflict creates stressful feelings for you or makes you anxious, and you cope with this by avoiding it, you're training your brain to disconnect whenever anything feels uncomfortable for you. The only solution for any of this is to learn to get comfortable with the uncomfortable feelings and sensations, and to understand that although they are unpleasant, they won't kill you. Deception tells you that you can't tolerate uncomfortable feelings, but that's not true. You will be amazed at what you can tolerate, and you'll see this later when we talk about resiliency.

Deadly Deception

But make no mistake, the lies that deception engenders can make people very sick and can literally change the neurochemistry in the brain.[2] Research shows an astounding correlation between physical and mental illness and our thought-life—75 to 98 percent![3] Deception was hard at work in my beloved husband's mind, causing him to buy into all sorts of lies that eventually made him very sick. Severe depression and paranoia led him to take his life one fateful day in November of 2013.

While I'm certainly not suggesting that everyone who has negative thoughts and believes lies will become mentally ill, I am saying that all of us pay a price for not paying attention to how our thought-life is affecting us. This means hitting the pause button long enough to notice our inner life and to identify the wounded parts of ourselves that need healing. It also means taking the space needed to ask for and get help if things start going south.

Statistics alarmingly speak for themselves if we take a look at what is happening in our culture regarding stress and mental health (for more information see http://psychcentral.com /blog/archives/2014/02/25/how-stress-affects-mental-health/). Deception abounds, and the worst thing it has the power to do is to create shame in the human soul, as we will see more in detail later.

Thoughts of shame include things such as

- I'm not worthy
- I'm unlovable
- I'm not good enough
- I'm intrinsically flawed

It's no wonder we are seeing the rise of teen suicides, depressive and anxiety disorders across all age groups, the effects of bullying (not only in school but in cyberspace), increases in self-harming behavior, eating disorders, sexual promiscuity, and a general confusion about sexual orientation.

When and how do we get these messages? When we're young and most vulnerable. It's really quite an ingenious plan if you think about it. When we're little and in the greatest need of a safe and secure attachment to our parents, we believe anything and everything we're told, especially about who we are. Our family becomes the first picture we get about how to love and be loved, and what it means to feel—or not feel—the attuned compassionate presence of another. It's the first picture we get of marriage and relationship rules.

Childhood can be a positive experience for those of us who were told we were special, but for those who were fed a steady diet of neglect, abuse, criticism, or humiliation, it was quite a different story. Toxic thinking got wired in early, and deception grew strong roots. Beliefs took shape that said, "I'm unlovable, I'm not good enough, something is wrong with me." The effect? The heart begins to crack a little at a time, until one day we simply quit caring, or we turn to something to anesthetize the pain.

In all my years as a psychotherapist, sitting with the wounded and listening to their stories, I have come to understand a profound truth about deception and the breaking of the heart. *It all begins with a lie.*

"Apple?" Dearie

You've heard the story a million times. Garden. Woman. Snake. Tree. Apple. Eve blew it. She decided she wanted what the fruit provided more than she wanted God. Eve wasn't doomed the minute she ate the fruit; she was doomed the minute she bought into the *deception.*

If only Thinking

Believe the lie. Take the apple. Eat a bite. Presto! Everything will be perfect. You'll be beautiful. You'll be secure. You'll be happy. You'll be like God.

Eve did it, and so did the wicked queen in one of our favorite fairy tales, *Snow White.* There was envy. Jealousy. Powers of darkness. The desire to be the most beautiful. The belief that destroying the princess would bring security and the endless admiration of others. The fruit was enticing. But it was deadly. Lies always bring death.

That's because Satan is out to convince you to indulge in "if only" thinking. If only you had _____, you would be happy. If only you were _____, you would be successful. If only you could just do _____, you would be worthy of love. "If only" thoughts represent deficit thinking. In other words, you're operating out of the belief that you're lacking something that if you just had, you would be okay. That's the trap. The problem is that it never quite works out the way we think it will. It didn't for the wicked queen, and it didn't for Eve.

"If only" thoughts give rise to discontentment, disillusionment, and depression. If these "if only" lies are continually downloading on your home screen, start noticing how they are affecting your mood and general well-being. Just try it for a day, and that should provide ample reason for you to take the setting of your mind as serious business.

If we don't set our minds on the truth, the Enemy of our souls will set them for us. If we aren't deliberate about taking our thoughts captive, they will automatically default to the negative, just like a computer defaults to specific settings. If we don't pay attention to the lies that are being downloaded on the home screen of our minds moment-by-moment, nothing will ever change in our lives. Our brains will never grow new neuropathways, and we'll keep repeating the same self-defeating patterns that are keeping us stuck and miserable.

If deception always brings death, we need to stop it in its tracks. If we don't, there will be a hefty price to pay. Eve didn't see it. Adam didn't see it. And you and I too often don't see it. My husband didn't see it either when he took his life.

Stop for a moment and think about a time you were deceived. What caused you to realize the deception? Most likely it was the revelation of truth that exposed the deception. But believing the lie probably made you behave in ways that you wouldn't have if you had only known the truth. Let's face it: Eve would not have eaten the fruit if she had known she wasn't really going to get to be like God.

Remember, deception is the Enemy's most powerful weapon against us—and sometimes it's hard to recognize the deception because we desperately want the outcomes it promises. Using a computer analogy, just think about all the junk emails you get offering you ways to get rich, become successful, lose weight, stay young, be desired, or get noticed in a noisy world.

How do you know which ones will deliver what's promised and which ones are deceptive? You don't. You have to slow down (become self-aware) long enough to think, reason, research, and then respond. Whether we're talking about the lies we may be prone to believe or the dysfunctional thought patterns we need to notice, we have to train our brains to recognize the truth (God's truth) before we can spot the counterfeit (the lies).

What's Downloading?

Thoughts are automatic. They are being downloaded into our minds at rapid speed all day long, and most of us don't even notice the effects they are having on our mood and emotions. It's like your computer. You can be working away on a word document

Pop ups Thats me   Waste Book, etc
1. Look internet   Memory
2. Distracted
3. Order

THINK THIS NOT THAT

while the latest version of Adobe Reader is downloading quietly in the background. Or you can be getting Instant Messages while you're posting something on your Facebook page.

How about this—have you ever been working on your laptop and had pop-ups appear? Maybe you went to a website to get some information, and before you can find what you're looking for, here comes an ad or a pop-up asking you to opt in, buy something, or watch a clip. What are these pop-ups trying to do? Sell you something. That's how my client David got hooked. "Hey, friend, look at this! If only you had this, did this, bought this, looked like this, were desirable like this, you would be smarter, sexier, stronger, prettier, thinner, or more successful!" And we take the bait—hook, line, and sinker.

While all of this can be annoying, it's designed for a purpose—to get an emotional reaction. Pop-ups, commercials, advertisements, and marketing are designed to help you think less (be unaware) and feel more. Because our thoughts are instantaneous internal responses to the external events going on in our world, successful marketers want to make you feel good by creating certain associations with a product they are trying to get you to buy. They often use the "if only" lies mentality to guarantee that if you purchase their product, you'll have miraculous results.

What we don't see with our computers is what's going on in cyberspace while all this junk is downloading. Just like we don't see all the branches of the neurons firing, synapsing, and causing changes in our brain chemistry, depending on where we chose to set our minds.

Why is this important? Because we react to our thoughts without even noticing their effect on our brains. The thoughts we place our confidence in and accept as true become what I call our "set-in-stone" beliefs, and because we've seen that what we believe determines how we behave, we have to train our brains to pay

O. Steen
Rich
- Book
- Tape
- etc

28

closer attention. How do we begin? By learning to *notice* what's downloading on our home screens.

STOP and Mind Your Brain

To help us become more aware of our thought-life and how it's impacting us, I've come up with an acronym to help you mind your brain, using the word STOP. The first thing we need to train ourselves to become aware of when our brains are on computer overload (which is probably most of the time!) is to (**S**) *Stop* and *Slow down* our thought process.

If you're like me, thoughts are bombarding you at rapid speed all day long. Research says that we can have as many as fifty to seventy thousand thoughts a day![4] That's a lot to sift through. In a later chapter, we'll delve into more of the neurobiology of thoughts, but for now it's safe to say that the nature and the types of thoughts we think will radically impact our overall mood.

The other word that will be important to associate with the (**S**) in our acronym is *Skill.* We're going to learn some new skills, and we're going to implement them in our daily lives because they work. Learning to cultivate deeper awareness is a skill you can learn and practice. The skills you will learn in this book will help you monitor your bodily state, your internal world, your relationships, and the world around you. Cultivating these skills will greatly enhance your emotional well-being and help you live a happier life.

The (**S**) will also serve as a reminder that practicing these skills will, in time, change the *Structure* of our brains. We will talk more about this concept, but for now, simply remember that to stop thinking "*That*" (old toxic thoughts) and begin thinking "*This*" (positive thoughts), you will need to rewire the neuro-networks in your brain. As neuroscientific research has proven, learning to focus our attention mindfully is the key to growing new neuro-networks. To recap:

[handwritten: v not what you think you are, what u think you are]

S reminds us to:
- **Stop** and **Slow down**—which will allow the
- **Skills** we've learned to accomplish the
- **Structural** changes in our brains

Testing Our Thinking *[handwritten: PR. 23:7]*

Slowing down our thinking will give us space to (**T**) *Test* our thoughts. The Bible says, "As he [man] thinketh in his heart, so is he" (Prov. 23:7 KJV). This has greater significance than you can imagine on a neurobiological level. As we think, our brains form different proteins. These proteins are what form our thoughts. God wasn't messing around when he repeatedly told us what to do about our thought-life. He knew the power a simple thought can have over us when we take it into our heart and believe it.

[handwritten: Meta highway] It may be helpful to think of the neuro-networks in your brain as highways, much like the roads we drive on. Each time you have a thought like, "I'm fat," the workers in your brain begin to dig a dirt road that says, "Yep, I'm fat all right." Every day you ruminate about that thought. You say it over and over in your mind, maybe hundreds of times a day. On a neurobiological level, neurons that fire together wire together, so now the highway workers are digging at breakneck speed, carving out these super-highways in your brain.

They're digging deeper and deeper until they're ready to lay the cement down on that thought, which by now is a set-in-stone belief. Once it's in cement, your brain will always default to it. Because of neuroplasticity, this can be changed. We can learn specific key intervention strategies for change, but it will require hard work, perseverance, and practice.

It's important for us to test the veracity of our thoughts. All of us have experiences that have affected us. For some of us, those have been predominately positive; for others, they've been quite negative—even traumatic. Whatever our life experiences have been, the meanings we have attached to them have helped create our thoughts and belief systems. Even though our perceptions or beliefs may be incorrect, we hold fast to what we have been taught or what we've learned.

Take Beth, for example. She was a perfect example of how thoughts left untested can have a disastrous effect on our lives. Beth came into my office as a successful businesswoman who was emotionally shut down. The reason she came for therapy was that out of the blue, she had begun to experience anxiety attacks. She told me this was very uncharacteristic because she never felt much emotion about anything. After having seen her physician for a medical evaluation, which proved inconclusive, she was advised to seek therapy.

As she told her story, I began to understand why Beth felt "so dead inside," as she put it. Unresolved attachment wounds from her past had filled Beth's mind with toxic thoughts. The problem was that it was hidden beyond her sense of conscious awareness.

Beth's mother left when she was only two years old. Her father was emotionally distant. When Beth was five, he remarried. Her stepmother was cold and detached. Beth's father had two other children with his new wife, and Beth was left feeling invisible and alone. As time went on, her stepmother became increasingly harsh toward her, favoring her two other children. As Beth sat in my office, a crystalizing moment occurred for her as she related the following story.

"It was as if something snapped inside me that day," Beth said. "It wasn't like what she said was any worse than any other time, but maybe I'd had enough. Right then and there as I stood in the kitchen listening to her belittling diatribe, while my father stood by silently, I swore I would never let them or anyone else get close enough to hurt me again. I was done being hurt. It's like I made a vow or something, and I didn't even realize it."

Beth took all these painful life-messages that she received from her mother's abandonment, her father's detachment, and her stepmother's cruelty, and attached meaning to them in regard to her self-worth. In her eyes, she came up empty. She was a loser.

Deep down in the recesses of her soul, Beth believed she was unlovable. Something must be wrong with her to be so sorely rejected by the people who were supposed to love her unconditionally. In order to compensate for her feelings of inadequacy, Beth poured herself into her schoolwork and never looked back. She became a straight-A student, got into a prestigious law school, and became a successful businesswoman. She learned how to get from her performance the value and worth she so desperately needed.

Beth's strategy worked for quite a while. The problem was that she never processed any of her losses: her mother's abandonment, her dad's indifference, and her stepmother's rejection. It took another difficult life incident for all that she had buried to come boiling to the surface. Beth had been running at breakneck speed, trying to avoid and bury the hurts from her past. In order to do that successfully, she had to "shut down" emotionally.

That day in her parents' kitchen when she made the vow to never let anyone hurt her again, it was an attempt to adapt to the loss of the love and affection she needed to survive. Beth erected a wall around her heart to protect herself from pain, rejection, and the fear her feelings stirred up.

The first thing we worked on was getting Beth to (**S**) slow down and begin to develop some self-awareness in her body. I taught her how to do a body scan and some breathing and focusing exercises (more on that later) to begin with. These would help to slow her down and calm her overactive emotional brain. As she attuned to her physical body, my hope was that she would begin to strengthen the parts of her brain that she had shut down—those parts that had not allowed her to feel.

T reminds us to:

- **Test** our thoughts

Observation Is Key

The next letter in our acronym, (**O**), is for *Observation*. I taught Beth how to increase her consciousness by learning to pay attention to her internal states. And, by learning to direct and focus her attention, she was changing the firing patterns of her own neurons. Later I'll be teaching you some specific focusing techniques that will increase your mental awareness.

I wanted Beth to pay attention to how often during her day she had feelings of anxiety. Then, I wanted her to pay attention to how her body felt when she experienced it. Did she tense up her muscles? Did she feel a knot in her stomach? Did she feel shaky? I asked her to spend ten minutes twice a day scanning her body from head to toe for tension. All these activities would increase her self-awareness about her emotional and physical states, and the focused attention would again help in the rewiring process.

We want to (**O**) *Oppose* and *Offer up* evidence to refute the veracity of toxic thoughts, because they can throw us off balance. They can be accusatory, condemning, and shaming. That's exactly what the Enemy of our souls desires. If he can throw enough junk mail at us and we buy into it, he's got us checkmated.

Taking one of Beth's false beliefs—"I'm unlovable"—I challenged her to offer up some evidence to support that statement. She told me the fact that her mom left her meant she was unlovable. "Okay," I said. "Has anyone ever loved you? "Well, yes," she replied, "my husband. My kids." "Okay, so what you're saying is you're not totally unlovable right?" "I never thought about it like that," she said, "but I suppose so." To recap:

O reminds us to:
- **Observe**
- **Oppose** toxic thoughts, and
- **Offer up** evidence to refute them

Practicing Makes Perfect

Finally, we have to (**P**) *Practice* these skills. We have to actively *Participate* in this process. In addition, we have to *Ponder* the truth and reject the toxic thoughts. That means we have to set our minds on, become conscious of, contemplate, and "think on" the truth *God* has given us. We've learned that focusing our attention will be a key element in making integrative changes in our brains. As Christians, we can be assured that the object of that focus (Christ) is rooted in truth. When we ponder God's truth about who we are and how much he loves us, we not only feel good, but we change our brain chemistry too.

For Beth, this meant coming to understand that she was lovable in God's eyes, no matter how "unlovable" she sometimes felt. This is what faith is all about. Faith is only as meaningful as the substance it is attached to, and our faith is built on a solid and firm foundation, Christ. The end result will afford us the ability to calm ourselves, regulate emotional responses, and achieve greater balance and harmony in our lives.

Practice is an action word. If we don't practice setting our minds, the Enemy of our souls will set them for us. "Practice makes perfect" is no joke here. The more you learn to cultivate awareness and become skilled at paying attention to what you're paying attention to, the easier it will be for you to learn to label your own internal world.

In time, you will become skilled at stopping toxic thoughts; you'll be able to test them in light of God's truth; you will be able to offer up or examine the evidence that would support or refute your negative claims, and learn to ponder (reflect or become conscious of) what's really true in your heart (according to God's Word).

P reminds us to:
- **Practice** the skills we'll learn so we can actively
- **Participate** in the process and
- **Ponder** the truth and reject the deception

I ask my clients to do specific exercises each day for six weeks to help them establish these new patterns. I find that if they are willing to be intentional about practicing these new skills, after the six-week period it becomes second-nature for them. They find in time that not only does it get easier, it actually makes them feel better. Negativity lessens, neural networks are being rewired, and freedom begins to come.

NOTES

[1] David Perlmutter, "Neurogenesis: How to Change Your Brain," *Huffpost*, updated May 25, 2011, http://www.huffingtonpost.com/dr-david-perlmutter -md/neurogenesis-what-it-mean_b_777163.html.

[2] David J. Abbott, "Zero Tolerance to Negativity: How to Create a Positive Brain," *Positive Buzz*, accessed October 17, 2017, http://positivebuzz.com /how_to_create_a_positive_brain.html.

[3] Caroline Leaf, "You Are What You Think: 75–98 Percent of Mental and Physical Illnesses Come from Our Thought Life!" *Dr. Leaf* (blog), posted November 30, 2011, http://drleaf.com/blog/you-are-what-you-think-75-98-of -mental-and-physical-illnesses-come-from-our-thought-life/.

[4] "Thoughts," Subliminal Pro Audio, https://subliminalpro.com/thoughts/.

Chapter Two

HARDWIRED: CHANGE YOUR THOUGHTS TO CHANGE YOUR BRAIN

For you created my inmost being; you knit me together in my mother's womb. I praise you because I am fearfully and wonderfully made.

—Psalm 139:13–14

In the previous chapter, I mentioned that Proverbs 23:7, "As a man thinketh in his heart, so is he," has greater neurobiological significance than we might realize. That's because while our thoughts may seem random, the systems at work behind the scenes forming them are anything but simple, and they influence every part of our being. Our brains are hardwired through these complex systems that are intimately involved in ordering our thinking and our behavior. God knew that how we think and what we set our minds on would have powerful implications not only on our hearts, but also on our neurochemistry.

Brain Science 101

Dr. Caroline Leaf, in her book *Switch on Your Brain*, says that thinking activity is real, and it can be seen on various types of brain imaging. She says the power of mind activity from simply reading a few lines on a page generates electromagnetic, electrochemical, and quantum action in your neurons. So, on a simplified level, if you have a toxic thought, the resulting proteins look different and act differently than if you had a healthy thought.[1]

Furthermore, this combined activity sets up an intricate and organized sequence of actions of neurotransmitters, proteins, and energy that forms a signal. Your thinking has just created a powerful signal that is going to change the landscape of your brain.[2]

So—think this through—if you have a toxic thought, your neurons, proteins, and all the other stuff going on in your brain to form that thought are going to look, act, and cause you to behave very differently than if you set your mind on what is pure, lovely, and of good report (Phil. 4:8). Are you tracking with me here? That's why that scripture in Proverbs is so powerful. As you think, so your neuropathways are wired—quite literally!

While I don't want to devote an entire chapter to the complex functioning of each part of the brain, it is necessary that we spend some time understanding the basics of this unique organ and what makes us different from other species. I encourage you to take your time and let this sink deep. These are scientific facts that have been empirically validated by years of research. Brain neurobiology is serious business, and it is the key to setting us free from toxic thinking. So, get excited and let's do this!

The Brain Is *Not* the Mind

Before we jump into dissecting brain parts, at the outset I'd like to clarify something important. The brain is *not* the same thing as the mind. Until I started to become interested in interpersonal neurobiology, and the work of Dr. Daniel Siegel and others, I used the words *mind* and *brain* interchangeably, as do many clinicians in the therapeutic world. I have come to learn they are very different concepts.

First of all, I can state the obvious, the brain is an organ and the mind is not. The brain is a physical structure located in the skull where the mind resides. Siegel says the mind is embodied, relational, and self-organizing. He provides the following definition in his book, *Mindsight*: "The human mind is a relational and embodied process that organizes the flow of energy and information."[3]

What does that mean? According to Siegel, it means that knowing that our mind regulates the flow of both energy and information enables us to feel the reality of these two forms of mental experience, and then to react on them rather than get lost in them.[4] In a later interview, he explains:

> The mind is this emergent aspect of a complex system. . . .
> [A]nd the system we're talking about is energy and
> information flow within us and between us. We realize
> that the mind is not just in the skull. And it's not just
> limited to the skin. The mind is . . . embodied. But it's
> also relational. . . . But if you really see the mind as both
> embodied and relational and as a self-organizing process,
> what is it doing? It's regulating energy and information
> flow within you and between you.[5]

Another important distinction about the mind that Siegel explains is this: "As a self-organizing emergent process, you can actually show scientifically why integration, the linkage of differentiated parts [of the brain], is actually the pathway to optimal self-organization. What does that mean? It means that non-integrated states are either *chaotic* or *rigid*" (italics mine).[6]

Siegel points out that in every mental health disorder (these are coded and explained in the Diagnostic and Statistical Manual for Mental Disorders—DSM–5), the complex system of the brain moves in one of two directions: toward *chaos* or *rigidity*. We can look at any disorder in the DSM–5 and find either or both of these present.

A depressive disorder would be an example of a rigid system, whereas an anxiety or panic disorder would exemplify a chaotic brain system. We'll talk later about techniques that will help with right- and left-hemisphere integration, but for now let's learn a little about the different parts and functions of our brain so that we can understand the impact of our thoughts.

Brain Explorer

There are three areas that make up the brain: the brainstem, the limbic area, and the cortex. The brain is divided into two halves, right and left hemispheres. For neural integration (defined as "the process of summation which then affects the process of neuron firing") to occur, the functional linkage of both sides must occur.[7] Knowing and understanding the basic functions of these brain regions will be important as we learn about how we can create the desired linkage through focused attention.

First up is the cortex. The frontal cortex allows us to think and reason. The prefrontal cortex area (PFC) is located at the top of the brain. Think of this part of your brain as the CEO or administrator of all that is uniquely you. The prefrontal cortex helps you process information that's coming in, controls your impulses, and helps you make decisions and stay focused. If this part of your brain is running low on gas, you'll see problems with self-regulation, planning, and the inability to pay attention to tasks. The prefrontal cortex plays a key role in the conscious focus of attention, which for our purposes is going to be the key to rewiring our brain.

This makes sense if you think about the symptoms of Attention Deficit Hyperactivity Disorder (ADHD). People who are ADD or

ADHD have lower levels of the neurotransmitters dopamine and norepinephrine, making finding and maintaining necessary stimulation difficult. Stimulant medications like Adderall strengthen this area of the brain by releasing dopamine, normally found in functional levels in the cortex. When the cortex is underactive, it is also believed that this area may not be able to efficiently use these chemical messengers or that the area has too few dopamine receptors available that connect the upper brain to the lower. How important is the PFC area of the brain to our thought-life? Let's take a look.

Luke came to my office because he was struggling with Post Traumatic Stress Disorder (PTSD) symptoms. He had been in Vietnam for two tours, and he witnessed a number of traumatic events. When he came home from the war, he was especially triggered by sounds and smells. Whenever he would hear popping noises (like fireworks on the Fourth of July), he would freak out. It took him right back to the traumatic memories of his friends being killed on the battlefield.

What happened to Luke in these moments? The alarm system in his brain (amygdala) went off and released adrenaline from his adrenal glands to alert him to possible danger. This triggered his administrator (prefrontal cortex—PFC), which immediately evaluated the situation and the source of the noises. If Luke's PFC concluded there was no real danger (it's just fireworks), he could calm himself down. The problem was that when he was under stress and pressure, his cognitive performance fell apart due to the release of increased levels of dopamine in the prefrontal cortex and the overstimulation of his limbic brain.

This caused his working memory and performance to take a nosedive. When the prefrontal cortex shuts down, executive functioning does too. If Luke saw a man with a gun, he often dropped back into the traumatic memories of Vietnam. This would cause his alarm system to get even louder, releasing more and more stress hormones into his bloodstream.

Luke's brain recorded the traumatic experiences he witnessed. This connected his neurocircuitry to the related memories from Vietnam and any present-moment triggers. It's easy to see how one can get stuck in toxic thinking when logic and the ability to reason go out the window and the brain's emotional center becomes highly activated and takes over. All of this caused Luke to experience the full-force sensory flow of a flashback and therefore not to be aware that this was something from his past. Luke reacted as if it were actually happening in the moment.

The truth is that even mild uncontrollable stress can cause a profound loss of cognitive abilities for a person with this kind of PFC damage. Prolonged stress exposure can cause structural changes in prefrontal dendrites. Again, the good news is that even in spite of these architectural changes, the brain can rewire by learning how to intentionally redirect thoughts.

Motor Systems

The basal ganglia are a group of interconnected structures deep within the cerebral cortex of the brain. They affect motor control. When the basal ganglion works too hard, we can feel anxious, panicked, and fearful. All these feelings are disastrous for our thought-life. In an article published through the Dana Foundation, Kayt Sukel says:

> Thanks in part to more sophisticated neuroimaging techniques, researchers have found that the basal ganglia are active in far more than movement. . . . The basal ganglia are involved not only with Parkinson's disease but also an array of psychiatric and addiction

disorders. Neuroimaging studies have shown abnormal activation of the striatum and other areas of the basal ganglia in patients with schizophrenia, attention-deficit/ hyperactivity disorder (ADHD), Tourette's syndrome, obsessive-compulsive disorder (OCD), and anorexia nervosa, as well as drug addiction.[8]

It's clear from neuroimaging studies that the basal ganglia area is responsible for a lot more than just movement. This structure is, in fact, responsible for integrating feelings with movement. It can calm or accelerate motor behavior. It can go into overdrive like a car that's idling too fast and needs to be recalibrated to the proper speed. When anxiety takes center stage in the limbic brain, it's easy to default to negative thinking. What this looks like in everyday life is that we get stuck in worry and trying to predict outcomes— generally worse-case scenario outcomes.

Later we'll talk more about the specific cognitive distortions we make, but for now, it's important to remember that people who tend to be pessimistic, predict negative outcomes, and live in the "what ifs" of life are using the distortion of *fortune telling*. Learning to overcome anxiety and the tendency to predict negative outcomes is critical to healing this part of your brain. That's what I helped Patty to see.

Patty came to my office wounded and broken. She had been disappointed by just about everyone in her life, so she was always waiting for "the other shoe to drop." She didn't realize it, but somewhere along the line she had made a vow to never let anyone get close enough to hurt her. She felt that if she didn't expect anything of anyone, she could protect herself from being hurt again. Patty wasn't consciously aware of how the deeper parts of her story affected her thinking.

In their book *The Relational Soul: Moving from False Self to Deep Connection*, Richard Plass and James Cofield explain why this occurs:

> Many people don't really know their story. Here is one reason why. Our story is composed of three things— events, (what happened), emotions (surrounding the events we experienced), and interpretations (what we think we learned from the events and emotions of our lives). Events and emotions don't become a story without interpretation. Our interpretation is the script of our lives. It becomes my identity, and I become my interpretation. For example, if I suffered a great deal of significant losses in my life (events) and felt a lot of sadness over those losses (emotion), it could be easy to decide I'm not going to ever get too close to anyone or anything because it's not safe (interpretation). My identity would be that of an aloof person.[9]

Relating this back to brain neurobiology and toxic thinking, we find that the brain holds both implicit and explicit memory. Explicit memory includes the things in our conscious awareness that we can readily pull up at any given time. Take riding a bike, for example; you can probably remember learning how to ride and recall a few falls and scrapes that you took. The falls might be something you can remember and call up at a given moment. Implicit memory allows you not to have to think too hard to get on the bike years later and ride; you just hop on and ride effortlessly. You don't have to remember how to balance or be coordinated, because all that is stored in your implicit memory. They are not visual memories but are tied to unconscious muscle memory. Explicit memories are memories we use every day, such as remembering a doctor appointment, recalling information for a test, or remembering your address.

Examples of implicit memory would include the ability to call up the words to an old song, drive your car, or type on your computer. We don't purposefully try to recall these things, so they get stored in our unconscious memory. The events and experiences in our lives, as well as the emotions attached to them, are also things we can recall pretty easily.

While Patty could call up specific events such as being abandoned by her father and being betrayed by her husband (explicit memories), what she wasn't consciously aware of was that her story was also held in her implicit memory, a place out of her conscious awareness. Things such as how she learned to do relationships, how she learned to love and be loved, what she thought about her intrinsic worth—all of these were being hardwired into her core self, deep beneath her conscious awareness.

This is where Plass and Cofieled's third component of interpretation comes in. Our interpretation of life-events affects our relationships both for good and for bad because they are translated into belief systems that we unconsciously choose to live from. Remember David from Chapter One? After digging deeper into his story, I uncovered a major soul-wound in his past that he had buried for years deep below his conscious awareness.

This wound, and the belief it fostered, were wired into Dave's implicit memory. It sat dormant for decades because it created shame. Left unaddressed, it reared its ugly head in his porn addiction. The soul-wound was the hidden part of Dave's story that needed linkage in his conscious awareness to be healed. In order to find freedom for our hearts and our brains, we must get to the core of both implicit and explicit memories.

For my client Patty, it became essential that we connect the dots between her conscious and unconscious memories. We had to move her implicit memories of how she learned to do relationships into her conscious mind. This was accomplished through the telling of her story in a secure and safe environment with me as her therapist.

Later, as she connected her story to the larger story of redemption that God was telling, she was able to relearn some new relationship rules. Patty's life story was one of redemption too, even though she didn't see it at first, and God wanted to use it to touch the hearts and lives of others within her circle of influence.

Telling her story to someone who was emotionally attuned and available to her gave Patty the opportunity to experience something different. Experience is what changes the physical structure of the brain through neural firing. As Patty told her story and I was able to resonate with it, she felt known. This is possible because of something called "mirror neurons." They allow us to feel other people's feelings. This is the foundation for empathy. It also explains how we are healed within the context of a safe, loving relationship.

Because Patty had never learned to label her own internal world, because she never understood that relationships were safe, loving, and secure, it was difficult for her to experience God's love. Once she was able to see herself as God saw her, she was able to reinterpret her story in light of his plan for her future, his love for her, and his beliefs about her value and worth. It's so important to understand that while implicit memories are not consciously recalled, they can have a profound influence on our behavior because they are at the core of relational memories, unconsciously influencing our past and future attachments.

To reinterpret our stories means we have to look at our sin and our suffering and decide some things about life, God, and the world around us. Plass and Cofield weigh in here beautifully:

Is this not the invitation of the gospel? We can own up to who we really are in the presence of God, who loves us beyond all measure. We can repent and surrender our false-self strategies to the One who lived, died, was raised and ascended to heaven. As we do, both initially and daily, the interpretation of our story changes. And when our interpretation changes, *so does our identity.*[10] (italics mine)

Emotions. Can We Trust Them?

When we talk about parts of the brain system that are responsible for our emotions and behavior, the most familiar one to most of us is the fight-flight-or-freeze response that takes place deep in the limbic system of the brain. A small almond-shaped mass of nuclei in the temporal portion of the brain called the *amygdala* is responsible to warn us of impending danger and set the alarm. The amygdala is involved in the processing of emotions such as fear, anger, and pleasure. It also determines what memories are stored and where. Experts think this determination is based on how monumental our emotional response is to an event.

When a stressful or traumatic event occurs, it affects the amygdala, the hippocampus, and the prefrontal cortex. The amygdala sounds the "danger" signal, and the body goes into one of three modes: fight, flight, or freeze. In his book *The God Shaped Brain*, Dr. Timothy Jennings explains it this way:

When the fire alarm is activated, the amygdala's job is two-fold: first to grab the attention of everyone in the building, and second to alert the 911 operator. Like a fire alarm, the amygdala both releases attention-getting adrenaline from the adrenal glands to the brain, and it alerts a sort of 911 operator to send out an urgent call.

The brain's 911 operator is the *Hypothalamus*, which is connected to the "radio tower" of the pituitary gland. Instead of radio waves, the pituitary gland transmits hormonal signals calling for the body's emergency response, which comes from the adrenal glands; they're the stress hormones know as glucocorticoids. After the alarm sounded, the brain's administrator, which is the dorsolateral prefrontal cortex (PFC), . . . evaluates whether there is real danger or whether it was a false alarm. If the administrator determines there is real danger, the alarm gets louder; if there's been a "false alarm," everything calms down.[11]

The other interesting thing about the limbic area is that it is the center for connection and for how we become emotionally attached to one another. The limbic area plays a regulatory role through the hypothalamus, the endocrine control center. Using the pituitary gland as its messenger, the hypothalamus sends and receives hormones throughout our bodies, influencing our sex organs, thyroid glands, and adrenals.

When we are stressed out, for example, we secrete a hormone that stimulates the adrenal glands to release cortisol, which mobilizes the body for the fight-or-flight response. This is great because it allows us to prepare for danger and gives us lots of energy. But high doses of cortisol can be toxic to our system and can negatively affect the growth and function of neural networks.

Your Brain on Lies

Let's set up a real-life scenario of how this might work if you encountered a stressful or fear-provoking situation in which your thinking went crazy. I want to tie this together to show you how what you tell yourself and what you believe to be true (even if it's not) affect how the brain, which is designed to rewire itself based on the thoughts we think, will degenerate. Here is our scenario:

You've been married for thirty-seven years. You've had a good relationship with your husband. You also trust one another. Now imagine that your best friend tells you she saw your spouse having a late-night dinner with another woman at a fancy hotel. Furthermore, she tells you your husband was trying on what looked like a ring on the woman's finger. You've been feeling insecure lately because your husband has been working late hours, and you've gained weight and feel unattractive.

How your brain processes the information your friend discloses first depends on whether you believe what she's telling you. Remember, your actions and reactions always follow your beliefs. Once you're sold that she's telling the truth, your reactions from a neuroscientific perspective will look like this: your prefrontal cortex activates the danger center (amygdala) in your limbic brain triggering anxiety, fear, and insecurity.

Now your primary goal becomes protecting yourself. You react by fleeing (flight) the room in tears. You can't think clearly. Your ability to make wise choices goes out the window, because your prefrontal cortex has lost the ability to think rationally and the emotional center of your brain has totally taken over. Because the danger signal is so powerful and produces such powerful emotions, your rational thinking ability is dramatically reduced.

At this point, toxic thinking sets in. Every bad relationship you have ever experienced comes flooding into your mind. Every hurt your spouse has ever put you through is magnified. Anger and rage flood your soul, and the pain of suffering crowds your conscious. No wonder you can't get a grip.

In order to be able to process this information rationally and not overreact, you first have to calm down your sympathetic nervous system. Think of this as the gas fueling your central nervous system. That's easier said than done because, as you can see, all these brain systems are working against you. But it can be done. We can learn to switch on peace—even in a situation like this one.

We do this by *choosing* to switch on the stress-control gene located in the hippocampus (part of the limbic brain system). If we're going to calm ourselves, we have to engage the parasympathetic nervous system. Think of this system as the brakes. We do this in various ways, but the first one is to control and calm the breath, as we will see later.

If we can do this during times of emotional stress and duress, we can begin to change our neurocircuitry. Once your PFC is back online, you decide to talk to your husband about what your friend disclosed, only to learn he had met up with your cousin who is a jeweler to buy you a surprise twenty-year anniversary band, and she was trying on the ring for him so he could see how it would look!

What Is Neuroplasticity?

When was the last time your brain worked out? Yes, your brain. Your brain needs exercise just like your body to improve its neuroplasticity—that is, its ability to make connections between neurons during your lifespan. Historically, it was believed that the brain was essentially unchangeable, that its structures were fixed and static and couldn't change past adulthood. If injury occurred, the brain could not repair itself. Over the last couple of decades, though, literally oceans of research have disproved this theory.

In 2000, neuropsychiatrist Eric Kandel won the Nobel Prize in neuroscience for proving that the brain is not entirely hardwired with fixed neuronal circuits.[12] This has led to many medical advances, including changing the way we treat brain injuries, mental illness, stroke victims, Parkinson's disease, and mental degeneration in diseases such as Alzheimer's. Furthermore, he demonstrated how experience creates new neural connections in the brain.

Attachment theory, pioneered by Dr. John Bowlby, had already built a formidable body of empirical research on this idea, suggesting that it's through the attachment process (experience) between mother and child that a child's brain learns to organize itself. The messages children receive through the hundreds of daily interactions with a primary caregiver (mom/dad) literally shape their brains, their identities, their core-beliefs systems, and help them to learn to regulate their emotional responses. A child learns to see himself/herself through what he/she witnesses in parental responses.

In the late 1980s, Dan Siegel, who wrote the groundbreaking book *The Developing Mind*, connected the dots between neurobiology and this growing body of research on attachment theory when he came across Bowlby and Mary Ainsworth's work. He was fascinated not only about *what* happened to individuals as children that shaped their brain, but *how* they came to make sense of what happened to them. This is what he believed predicted their emotional integration as adults. Siegel wondered what the neurobiological workings of the brain were that made attachment so important, and how one makes a coherent narrative happen in the brain.

All of this groundbreaking research on the brain—the concept of neuroplasticity and attachment theory—give us great hope in the field of psychotherapy. This information lends scientific fact to ideas that were almost laughable when Dr. Bowlby presented them back in his day to the then-equivalent of the American Psychiatric Association. This new research shows that we are not predestined from a bad beginning. In fact, according to attachment theory, a person can be *healed* through an emotionally attuned, loving, and compassionate relationship—at the neurobiological level.

To quote Siegel: "If you can make sense of your story, you can change it." He also believes that connections in the brain shape the way we think, but the flipside is also true. The way we think can change our brain: "Neural firing changes neural connections if we pay attention."[13]

What does all this mean for you and me? Simply that the story isn't finished yet. If we can learn to pay close attention to what we're telling ourselves, if we can be intentional and deliberate about our thought-lives, we can take advantage of this concept of neuroplasticity and really affect change in our brains and ultimately in our stories.

NOTES

[1]Caroline Leaf, *Switch on Your Brain: The Key to Peak Happiness, Thinking and Health* (Grand Rapids: Baker Books, 2013), Kindle.

[2]Leaf, *Switch on Your Brain.*

[3]Daniel J. Siegel, *Mindsight: The New Science of Personal Transformation* (New York: Bantam Books, 2011), 52.

[4]Siegel, *Mindsight*, 53.

[5]Daniel J. Siegel and Rick Hanson, "What Really Matters about Neuroscience," in a virtual conference on Psychology Networker, 2013, http://www.psychotherapynetworker.org/CEcourses/webinars/brain_science/Session6_Siegel-Hanson.pdf.

[6]Siegel and Hanson, "What Really Matters about Neuroscience."

[7]Pam Nugent, "Neural Integration," Psychology Dictionary, http://psychologydictionary.org/neural-integration/#ixzz3wKL2QWaG.

[8]Kayt Sukel, "Brain Work: Basal Ganglia Contribute to Learning, but Also Certain Disorders," The Dana Foundation, January 2007, http://www.dana.org/Publications/Brainwork/Details.aspx?id=43646#sthash.B6DB9cvl.dpuf.

[9]Richard Plass and James Cofield, *The Relational Soul: Moving from False Self to Deep Connection* (Downers Grove, IL: Intervarsity Press, 2014), 99–100.

[10]Plass and Cofield, 101.

[11]Timothy R. Jennings, *The God Shaped Brain: How Changing Your View of God Transforms Your Life* (Downers Grove, IL: Intervarsity Press, 2013), Kindle.

[12]Edythe McNamee and Jacque Wilson, "A Nobel Prize with Help from Sea Slugs," CNN, updated May 14, 2013, http://www.cnn.com/2013/05/14/health/lifeswork-eric-kandel-memory/index.html.

[13]Mary Sykes Wylie, "Mindsight: Dan Siegel Offers Therapists a New Vision of the Brain," *Psychotherapy Networker Magazine*, September/October 2004, 34–37.

✝ what Do we Tell ooRselves Ph.4.8

Chapter Three

HOOKED: OUTSIDE FORCES INFLUENCING THE MIND

I guess we're all two people. One in daylight,
and the one we keep in shadow.

—Bruce Wayne in *Batman Forever*

As we've seen from attachment theory, we are wired for relationship and secure connection from birth. When that need goes unmet, the attachment alarm system (the amygdala) goes off, and the need for secure connection becomes salient and compelling. In other words, we're motivated to seek closeness to the ones who can keep us safe. The problem is, life isn't always safe, and neither are the people in it.

A central tenet of attachment theory is that our attachment figure(s) are supposed to be a secure base and a safe haven. Opportunities to experience secure connection from our caregivers occur thousands of times during the first few years of life. These scenarios often unfold around emotionally charged events— from anger to anxiety and sadness. How a parent helps a child deal with his/her emotional responses around everyday life situations is critical because, as we've pointed out, the brain records these scenarios and draws conclusions about the self.

These will be important concepts to keep in mind as we talk later about specific cognitive distortions (thinking errors) we are all prone to make. You will come to understand how you could easily make the distortion of jumping to conclusions about what someone else is thinking or feeling about you if you've experienced a lot of negative messages about who you are from your significant caregivers. A steady diet of these negative life messages makes trusting people in general very difficult.

If we will take the time to become more self-aware about our stories, seeking to understand and make sense of them, we can discover some important information about ourselves—who we are, and why we think, love, and behave the way we do. Attachment theory provides a clear lens of understanding why we get "hooked" on these negative, toxic patterns of thinking. We buy into the recorded information we receive as kids, and we run with it.

A former client of mine is a great example of someone who got so entrenched in self-defeating thinking that it nearly destroyed her. Susan came to my office seeking help with an eating disorder. She loathed her body. She started out wanting to lose a few pounds because her father constantly made comments about her "thick" thighs. "A few pounds" soon became a few more, and before she realized what was happening, she landed in the hospital weighing a mere eighty-nine pounds although she was five-feet four-inches tall.

Susan spent years trying to fit in. As she shared her narrative with me, it became clear that she had endured years of being put down by her father, who spent much of his time objectifying women. She learned early on that to get a man, you had better be thin and pretty. Her dad never had anything positive to say to her.

By the time she was twelve, Susan had bought into the lie that she wasn't good enough. She dealt with the negative messages by constantly trying to please, to be perfect, and to stay in shape. Unfortunately, all those toxic messages about her self-worth were being encoded in her young brain, and because kids are the best recorders of information but the worst interpreters, Susan learned that to get the love and attention she needed, she had to please at all costs.

Doing things perfectly did a couple things for Susan. First, it calmed her over-active limbic brain, because according to Hebb's Law, the more she practiced behaviors such as pleasing, avoiding conflict, and stuffing her true feelings, her brain learned to associate those actions as calming, wiring them in as everyday habits. Susan could avoid the painful feelings of anxiety through her try-hard behavior, but it was only a temporary respite. She was really only as good as her last performance. If she stopped being perfect, the anxious thinking and ruminating returned with a vengeance.

Susan's perfectionism came with an even heftier price: she never developed her authentic self. As she grew into adulthood, she felt lost. She was so busy pleasing everyone else that she didn't know herself. One thing was certain, the lies she had spent a lifetime believing and telling herself had left her miserable. She was clinically depressed from all the years of toxic thinking. Remember, all this mess lay below the conscious surface for Susan. All the things she was unaware of about her life and her story were keeping her stuck.

Payoffs

Do folks like Susan want to be miserable? No. Was she simply unaware of how her beliefs and negative internal monologues were affecting her? Absolutely. Just like Susan, the rest of us become stuck in negative patterns because we are deceived into

believing that we can't tolerate the anxiety that being authentic
and finding a voice would bring. Susan also wasn't aware of how
her larger narrative was impacting her belief system and her brain.

To cope and keep uncomfortable sensations at bay, Susan
opted for what had become familiar—never let anyone catch you
making a mistake. That way she could maintain a sense of control.
Unfortunately, that control was only an illusion. It only provided
temporary relief. Once Susan let down her guard, the anxious
thoughts came back with a vengeance.

I began our work with Susan by teaching her to begin paying
attention to her internal monologues. Every day, she was to record
how many negative things she told herself and how many anxious
thoughts she had. It was only then that she was able to see how
much power these toxic thoughts were having over her mind.

In her article "Negative Thinking: Can Thoughts Kill?," Dr.
Tiffany Johnson says that according to scientists, of our sixty thousand thoughts a day (one thought per second), 95 percent are the
same thoughts we had yesterday, and the day before, and the day
before that. Our minds are playing the same thoughts over and
over, which wouldn't be so bad if it weren't for the next statistic:
for the average person, 80 percent of those thoughts are negative.
If you do the math, this means that most of us have more than
forty-five thousand negative thoughts each day![1]

Toxic thinking leads to unhealthy behaviors in our everyday
lives. The key is noticing the connection between our thoughts
and our behaviors. In Susan's case, her thoughts—"I can't make a
mistake or I'll be rejected; I am fat and unlovable; if I'm not perfect, I'm not worthy of love"—led to eating-disordered behavior,
anxiety, and depression.

The Centers for Disease Control cites a significant link between
stress and six of the leading causes of death: heart disease, cancer,
lung ailments, accidents, cirrhosis of the liver, and suicide. Stress

58

makes us fat, causes illness and disease, and sends a large number of Americans to an early grave. Yes, stress will kill you, and negativity is a stressor you just don't need.[2]

By now you might be thinking, why would anyone in their right mind want to be negative or to think negative thoughts all day long? The answer is simple: most of us aren't *aware* and we don't see how our past controls what we tend to obsess about. We're doing it because it has become so natural, but whatever we ruminate about will grow until it takes over our thought-life. We'll become what we think about. It's like a garden. If you fertilize it and water it, the plants will flourish. If you don't remove the weeds on a regular basis, they will grow and take over your flowers.

People who suffer from anxious or depressive thinking are more prone to negative thinking and negative self-talk. The first thing you have to do is to become aware of your thought-life. I simply can't stress this point enough, because *you can't change what you don't pay attention to.*

What's the Hook?

When we think about our thought-life, we have to become aware of all the things that are impacting our thinking. In other words, what are the things out there for each of us personally that cause us to buy into these negative attributions about ourselves. My friend Dr. Greg Jantz says this in his book *Hooked: The Pitfalls of Media, Technology, and Social Media:* "We tend to lock our houses, deadbolt the doors, and bar the windows. We keep out tangible, understandable threats but often leave ourselves wide open to other kinds of dangers."[3]

What are some of these other dangers that may impact our thinking and drive our thought-life? One is social media. We all use it. We all love it. But are all of these sites we're connected to facilitating our authenticity, or are we creating a false self as we play virtual games? What in the world does that have to do with negative thinking patterns? Let's take a look.

Let's say you're single and want to meet someone. You don't want to hit the bar scene, so you decide to try online dating. You post your profile. When you post a profile on Match, or any other dating site, are you being real? Or are you creating a virtual self that leaves out all the stuff you don't want your potential match to know about you? Maybe you are being authentic, but how about the millions of other people out there? How do you know if they are hiding their true selves?

How about sharing posts on Facebook? Do we take extra care to post only the good stuff we're doing, the things that will make us look good to others? If so, why are we doing this? The answer is simple: we want to be liked. We want people to think we have it all together, and we don't want to face rejection.

Let's face it, we are living in a digital age, an age where people (especially our kids) are growing up communicating very differently with one another. Just because a lot of our communication isn't oral or face-to-face doesn't mean we don't ruminate about what people are posting, tweeting, Instant Messaging, saying on Facebook, or on Match.com. Is it possible that some of these things might be contributing negatively to our thought-life and to who we believe we are?

Here are some alarming statistics on just how much time and energy are devoted to thinking through the use of social media:

- Facebook has recorded 945 million active users on mobile devices, 757 million per day, and an astonishing 1.23 billion per month.[4]
- Fifty-seven percent of people report they talk to others more online than face-to-face.[5]

We spend a great deal of time creating a false self (digital identity) that can lead to thoughts of self-loathing and what Kelsey Sunstrum calls "smiling depression." In an article in *PsychCentral*, Sunstrum says:

> One factor for the high rates of depression seen in social media-friendly people is the inconsistency they observe between their ideal cyber self and their self-image. The desire to be seen positively has taught us to silence our troubles, and we now have no idea how to express inner turmoil without feeling like we're accepting social defeat.
>
> For obvious reasons, people do not advertise their negative traits on their social profiles, nor do they post unflattering pictures. Because of this strict control of the way we are viewed, we are often fooled into believing other people's lives are much better than our own. What is essential to remember is they too wear masks, the way I do, the way everyone does.[6]

In an interview, pediatric nurse Denise Daniels weighed in, saying that kids aren't learning to communicate face-to-face but through emails and texts, and it's having a significant effect on their brains: "'Technology can be a big hindrance on interpersonal relationships,'" Daniels says. "'For all its benefits, technology can completely rewrite a child's brain pathways in a very different way than how they would normally develop.'"

Daniels is talking about neurotransmitters—those chemicals in the brain that relay information between nerves. A developing child is born with pathways that expand based on stimulation like a parent's voice, music, touch, and eventually, play. They also help children file and organize endless pieces of information gathered as they age. But for children who spend too much time interacting through a screen, something happens, Daniels says. "'Their neural pathways change and different ones are created. It affects concentration, self-esteem, in many cases they don't have as deeply personal relationships. They lose empathy. We've seen kids like this that don't develop those sympathetic and empathetic skills they need.'"[7]

What does all this Internet and social media stuff have to do with toxic thinking and what we tell ourselves? Plenty. Social media is a very strong and powerful influence, as the above articles and statistics assert. Social Media can be good. It can also be bad. If you're still not convinced, take a look at cyberbullying and the effects it's having on the thought-life of kids today. Kaspersky Lab says, "Cyberbullying is the use of the Internet, mobile phones, and other technology to send or publish a textual or media content to hurt or offend another person."[8] This is accomplished through the following:

- Gossip—Public statement of speculation
- Exclusion—A group of friends sets themselves aside from one person
- Harassment—Constant and deliberate mockery
- Cyberstalking—Promises to bring conflict into real life
- Trolling—Provocation, implicit insult
- Comments—Negative responses to texts, photos, or videos
- Dissing—Permanent posting and messaging despite refusal to communicate
- Fake profiles—Creating fake accounts or profiles used to threaten victim
- Trickery—Posting other people's secrets and personal information

What does Kaspersky say are the negative consequences for kids as a result of this?

- Social—Loss of interest in communication; worse behavior at school; truancy
- Emotional—Aggressive behavior and depression; anxiety and fear; sullenness
- Physical—Suicide

More alarming statistics:

- Three million kids at least once a month miss school because of the threat of cyberbullying.
- Eight hundred thousand kids a year are the subjects of cyberbullying on Facebook.
- One out of five kids suffering from cyberbullying thinks about suicide.
- One out of ten attempt suicide.

A quick glance at your own techno-life may reveal to you that social media can have a very powerful and sometimes toxic effect on how you think about yourself and how others see you. Don't get me wrong, I love social media. It's just a vehicle. People will use it for good and for evil, but let's not just take the good and ignore the potential pitfalls of the bad. We would be very foolish not to take these statistics to heart if just one person takes their life over it.

If you're hiding behind a mask on social media sites or anywhere else, it's time to take it off and get serious about who you are. The only way to truly understand your value and worth is to find it in something bigger than you. Enter Jesus. So, put down the computer once in a while and read God's Word; let it define you; let truth take root in your brain and find your identity in who *he* says you are, not in what others think.

Are You Popular?

Think about it. What's the first thing you do when you wake up? Check your cell? Check your email? Log on to Facebook? Shoot out a tweet? Maybe you're playing Farmville! Maybe you're trying to find Mr. or Mrs. Wonderful, and you're on a few dating sites, and you need to check to see if anyone is interested in you today.

Did anyone say something about your profile? Did anyone even notice you? If not, think about how it makes you feel? I've talked to a lot of women who feel absolutely awful about themselves because they get no hits on their profile. Or the ones they do get are from people they would never be interested in. Their thoughts: *Something must be wrong with me. I'm not attractive enough. I'm not thin enough. I'm not interesting enough.*

You see where I'm going with this? It's all about the messages we receive, and social media is a place where we receive a lot of input about ourselves. If we're hooked on being popular, we'll hide our true self and create a well-controlled version of who we are, or who we want others to think we are, so that we can check off the boxes to say we're okay.

We become more and more entrenched in this false reality because we need our fix. What's the fix? It's getting those core needs met. Why do we want to be popular on a dating site or any other media? Because it makes us feel good when we get noticed. If we don't get enough likes, winks, smiles, hits, texts, IMs, or no one responds to our tweets, we may feel we're not special. It feels good to be popular, and it fuels our thoughts about who we are. Relating this back to brain biology, we know that when something feels good, it activates the pleasure centers in our brain. The more endorphins being released, the more "hooked" we are.

Start being aware of this. Try a simple experiment by paying attention to how you feel every time you hear that familiar *"ding"* signal when you're getting a text or a voicemail. How do you feel when you open your email and see your inbox is full? What's it like when you see that ten new potential admirers have asked to chat with you on Match? If you're excited, that means your dopamine reward circuits are turned on.

What do you do when you experience these things? Do you jump up right away to see who it is that texted you or left a voicemail? Do you stop and listen to the message? Do you check your inbox throughout the day? To test this out, I tried watching my friends one day as we were sitting around the table having lunch (I know, I do it, so I'm not off the hook). Every time the phone rang, or a text came through, they would get up and leave the group conversation to see who it was that messaged them. Botta Bing! Let's face it—we're all hooked. But let's take a closer look at what all this self-talk is doing to our psyches.

The Illusion

Amanda came to see me because she was having an affair that started online. She was lonely. Her hubby was gone a lot, and she started using Facebook more than usual. One day an old flame Instant Messaged her. They started chatting. After a few weeks, Amanda found herself looking forward to hearing from him, and she found herself checking her email constantly throughout the day. But she didn't pay attention to her thoughts. In fact, she used the cognitive distortion of minimizing them, telling herself that there was no harm in connecting with an old "friend." All she knew was that it felt good to get the attention.

Amanda's friend confided in her that he was having marriage problems and was headed for a divorce. Amanda began to notice that she wasn't talking about her husband or her kids anymore. Somehow a shift occurred, and this virtual world she was living in with her old boyfriend was taking her back to days gone by where she was popular, carefree, and twenty pounds lighter. She felt attractive again.

What was Amanda doing here? She was getting her needs met for value and worth. She was feeding the dopamine centers in her brain. She was imagining a make-believe life with a person she really knew nothing about. She was creating in her mind what she wanted him to be, but she didn't have to grind out the mess of everyday life with him.

That's the hook. That's the illusion. We can't ignore our real-life partners, kids, and problems, but online we can go anywhere with almost anyone. We create a virtual relationship where we can begin to reveal only what we want to about ourselves to make us more desirable. But sadly, the deeper we get into it, the more we disconnect from real-life relationships. The deeper we get, the more thinking errors we ignore.

Food and Fashion Go Together

The other two venues that radically affect our thought-life and hook us in are the two F's—the food and fashion industry. In 2013, U.S. citizens spent three hundred sixty-one billion dollars in retail sales and bought nineteen billion garments.[9] That's a lot of clothes. In 2013, the total sales for the beauty/cosmetic industry was four hundred twenty-six billion dollars.[10] What does all this mean? It means we care about how we look. Why? Because television, social media, magazines, the food industry, the fashion industry, and everything else out there has given us one message: you have to be thin, beautiful, smart, make money, and dress cool, or you don't measure up.

You may think you're not buying into all this stuff, but trust me, it's impacting how you see yourself and what you tell yourself. Here are a few simple questions to ask yourself to check the pulse on your heart:

- Do you buy the latest magazines and compare yourself or your body to celebrities? If so, why?
- Do you get Botox, or have you had plastic surgery? If so why?
- Do you have to be successful? If so, why?
- Do you have to be a perfectionist at whatever you do? If so, why?
- Do you color your hair? If so, why?
- Do you have to wear designer labels? If so, why?
- Do you watch what you eat? If so, why?
- Do you workout all the time? If so, why?
- Do you worry or ruminate about your weight? If so, why?
- Do you buy special cosmetics? If so, why?
- Do you keep up with the latest fashion trends? If so, why?
- Do you think a lot about how you look? If so, why?

These are just a few things to consider in what could be an exhaustive list. The real question is why are we doing any of these things? The answer is simple: not only do we care about how we look, we care about what people think about how we look. We care about the image. The messages out there have impacted our thinking. That's why we have commercials to sell us on the whole idea of beauty, fashion, and weight loss.

They tell us we need to look good, smell good, and be successful. All of us to some degree tell ourselves things about our appearance, our weight, our financial situation, our intelligence, and our sense of style. Start noticing how some of these so-called innocent things are affecting your thought-life and what you're telling yourself. The answers may surprise you.

Wait a minute, you may be thinking. Is it so terrible to care about these areas of our lives? No, not if we can keep it in perspective. Not if it doesn't become all-consuming, and not if we have a strong sense of who we are in God's economy. There is nothing wrong with wanting to look your best and be healthy, but when you can't think of anything else, there's a problem with your thought-life. How do we know if we're not on the right track? Glad you asked. Let's dig deeper.

Jenna was a former client of mine. She came to me because she had developed bulimia. Jenna wasn't fat, but she bought into the lie that, in order to get and keep a guy, she had to be thin and perfect. It started in high school when someone made a comment about her thighs. She was devastated. Right there and then she made a vow to herself that she would lose weight and trim down. She became obsessed with her body image and thought about food all the time. She spent most of her days worrying about how much she needed to exercise to burn off what she ate.

Jenna started dieting to lose a few pounds. No big deal. She lost ten, and she started getting some compliments on her appearance. It felt good. It met her needs for value, acceptance, security, and adequacy. Remember, Jenna already had a core belief that she had to be thin and perfect to get a man. That belief was substantiated with all the compliments she received for losing weight. Somewhere along the line something happened, and Jenna lost control. She was purging five times a day. She dropped thirty pounds. She was hospitalized and in serious condition.

When she was stable, I recommended to Jenna's family a treatment center for eating disorders. During her therapy there, it came out that Jenna had been molested when she was sixteen—something she had never told her family. The trauma had set in motion a self-destructive path for Jenna. She held on to the shame that it was somehow her fault. She believed she was worthless and no good, and no amount of telling her otherwise was going to change that until she came face to face with the One who is "the truth and the light," Jesus.

Jenna was very open to hearing about how much God loved her. In time, she was able to release her shame to a loving God. She was also able to see herself as more than the sum total of her appearance. She accepted that God loved and valued her enough to die for her and redeem her life. She knew she had been given a second chance. What started out as a diet to lose a few pounds turned into a monster that overtook Jenna's identity and held much greater meaning underneath the surface. This was true for Jenna and millions of others like her who struggle with eating disorders.

Through solid biblical counseling and an understanding of what it means to have her identity in Christ and not in the externals of life, Jenna recovered and is now working on her Master's in counseling to help other young women who struggle with disordered eating.

Check Your Pulse

By now you should be pretty convinced that you need to take an inventory of how outside forces have impacted your thought-life. If you've never paid attention to it, now is a good time to start. Begin to notice which of the categories we've talked about might be influencing you. Pay attention to what you're telling yourself. Record your findings in a journal for a week. Be honest with yourself and see if you're hooked. Your answers may surprise you.

NOTES

[1]Tiffany Johnson, "Negative Thinking: Can Thoughts Kill?," Healing Touch Chiropractic, accessed October 17, 2017, http://htchiro.com/negative -thinking-can-thoughts-kill/.

[2]Dr. Tiffany, "Negative Thinking."

[3]Gregory Jantz and Anne Murray, *Hooked: The Pitfalls of Media, Technology, and Social Media* (Lake Mary, FL: Siloam/Charisma House Book Group, 2012) Kindle.

[4]Emil Protalinski, "Facebook Passes 1.23 Billion Monthly Active Users, 945 Million Mobile Users, and 757 Million Daily Users," *The Next Web*, January 29, 2014, http://thenextweb.com/facebook/2014/01/29/facebook-passes-1-23 -billion-monthly-active-users-945-million-mobile-users-757-million-daily -users/.

[5]Alex Trumpe, "The World Is Obsessed with Facebook," YouTube, February 21, 2011, http://www.youtube.com/watch?v=x) XOavGwAW8&noredirect=1.

[6]Kelsey Sunstrum, "How Social Media Affects Our Self-Perception," *Psych Central*, March 14, 2014, http://psychcentral.com/blog/archives/2014 /03/14/how-social-media-affects-our-self-perception/5.

[7]Chandra Johnson, "Face Time vs. Screen Time: The Technological Impact on Communication," *Deseret News*, August 29, 2014, http://national .deseretnews.com/article/2235/Face-time-vs-screen-time-The-technological -impact-on-communication.html#BLR5ZYIdVLI4KgwZ.99.

[8]Kaspersky Lab, "Cyberbullying Facts," *Kid Safety*, September 21, 2015, http://kids.kaspersky.com/cyberbullying/parents/facts/.

[9]"Global Industry Fashion Statistics: International Apparel," *Fashion United*, accessed October 3, 2017, http://www.fashionunited.com/global-fashion -industry-statistics-international-apparel.

[10]"The World Spends Billions to Look Beautiful. How Big Is the Beauty Industry?," *FashInvest*, April 19, 2013, http://www.fashinvest.com/world -spends-billions-beautiful-big-beauty-industry/.

Chapter Four

IT'S JUST A THOUGHT—
ISN'T IT?

We demolish arguments and every pretension
that sets itself up against the knowledge of God,
and we take captive every thought to make it obedient to Christ.

—2 Corinthians 10:5

It is not what goes into the mouth that defiles a person,
but what comes out of the mouth; this defiles a person.

—Matthew 15:11 ESV

Sandy was pretty stressed out when she came to see me. She had a high-pressure job as the executive assistant to the CEO of a major corporation. Her boss was a "demanding ogre," in her words. She worked about seventy hours a week, and it was killing her.

One day, out of the blue, she was giving her boss an introduction before his speaking engagement when she froze in her tracks. Her mind went blank before a huge audience. She couldn't get her words out. Her heart rate started going through the roof. She felt shaky and started to sweat. She was humiliated. To make matters worse, her boss did not handle the situation with grace. In fact, he blasted her afterwards. That's when the dam broke.

Unlike Stella, Sandy couldn't get her groove back. Out of nowhere she would find her heart racing, her hands shaking, pressure in her chest, and she also had the sensation that she was

71

coming out of her body. She was afraid to do anything for fear that another episode would overtake her. After five different trips to the ER for other stress-related incidents and to make sure she wasn't having a heart attack due to the pressure in her chest, and after being assured repeatedly that she was fine, Sandy decided to seek out therapy.

I told her she wasn't going crazy. She was experiencing panic attacks, very frightening and uncomfortable experiences, but not dangerous. Sandy was relieved but still worried. "I still can't function," she retorted. "I'm a mess. I'm never going to get over this, and I'm going to lose my job. If I do, I'll lose everything and I'll be on the streets!"

Sandy was making the cognitive distortion of catastrophizing. She already had herself jobless, in the poorhouse, and on the homeless scene. I told Sandy that what she needed was a crash course in brain neurobiology and a little psycho-education about Panic Disorder. She agreed to proceed. Panic is a great example to explain the powerful effects of our thoughts on our brains and our bodies. They really are just thoughts, but, as we've seen, they carry with them tremendous neurobiological power. Let's take a look at what would happen to Sandy when she perceived danger.

Panic is a natural response to impending danger. It's the built-in alarm system God wired us with. We've discussed the instinctual fight-or-flight reaction that we all have to physiologically prepare for danger when our survival is threatened, but with panic disorder, there is often no immediate threat; we simply attribute danger to the bodily sensations we're experiencing. That's what happened with Sandy. Her mind misinterpreted the symptoms in her body and perceived them as life-threatening. Her reactions included:

- Increased heart rate
- Increased respiratory rate

- Increase in blood flow to muscles to prepare to run like crazy or fight
- Shakiness
- Dizziness
- Sweating
- A sense of coming out of her body
- Increasing flow of adrenaline, cortisol, and other neurotransmitters

Sandy's body was going through the exact physiological fight-or-flight response that a person who was in real danger would experience, but there was no emergency, nothing life-threatening for her to fear. What makes this so maddening is that these reactions can appear to come out of the blue in the absence of any meaningful stimulus. That's what was crippling Sandy—fear of the unknown.

Breaking the Connection of Catastrophic Thoughts

Anxiety, panic, depression, and grief issues all have one thing in common—a mind-body connection. Whether we're talking about what someone says about us on social media, or we have a fear of snakes, or we have some type of chemical imbalance, it all boils down to this: whatever stress is felt in the soul will spill over into the body and cause physical health problems.

Sandy made a myriad of thinking errors that all of us can make when faced with panic. Here is how her mind/body connection went awry and how she misinterpreted her physical symptoms:

- Her pounding heart deceived her into believing she must be having a heart attack (hence all those visits to the ER)
- Her dizziness made her believe she would faint in front of all those people at the meeting (shame, embarrassment)

- Her feelings of de-realization (coming out of her own body) deceived her into thinking she must be going crazy and would have to be institutionalized
- Her shakiness made her believe she wouldn't be able to move off the podium to escape the danger

Using the psycho-education process, I taught Sandy that what she was telling herself was ramping up her fear response center. Once she realized that what her body was going through wasn't dangerous, that helped to dissipate her fears. I went over the above thinking errors with her one at a time. Let's take a look.

Panic attacks do not cause heart attacks.
An elevated heart rate during a panic episode can be scary, but it's not dangerous. Research has proved that during a panic attack there are no EKG abnormalities, only sinus tachycardia. A normal healthy heartbeat for adults is sixty to one hundred beats a minute. But your heart can beat up to 250 beats per minute without sustaining damage. I told Sandy that if her heart began to pound during an attack, let it rip, eventually it would calm down.

Panic attacks will not cause you to faint.
Sandy felt dizzy and lightheaded when she experienced an attack. She was terrified she would faint. That's because the blood circulation to the brain is reduced due to rapid breathing and hyperventilation. This is not dangerous and can be reduced by diaphragmatic breathing. The heart is pumping harder during an episode and increasing your circulation, so it's almost impossible to pass out.

You are not going crazy.
Because of the release of chemicals into the bloodstream and the central nervous system, the intense reactions in your body not only can be scary but they can make you feel as if you're coming out of your body (de-realization) or going crazy. You're not. Sandy was afraid she would totally lose it and become paralyzed, unable to move. The opposite is true. During a panic attack, your senses are experiencing hyperarousal with one goal in mind—escape! The out-of-body feeling will dissipate as soon as you calm down. It may leave you exhausted, but not crazy.

All the mistaken bodily cues, erroneous beliefs, and cognitive distortions Sandy experienced were ablated by understanding the brain-body connection and how the tendency to interpret uncomfortable bodily sensations in a catastrophic way leads to an overblown stress response. It looks something like this:

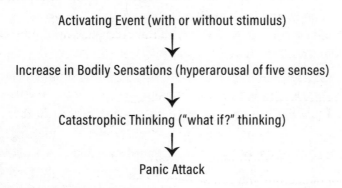

Activating Event (with or without stimulus)
↓
Increase in Bodily Sensations (hyperarousal of five senses)
↓
Catastrophic Thinking ("what if?" thinking)
↓
Panic Attack

I needed to help Sandy intervene in this negative cycle and help her increase her awareness of what she was telling herself in the moment. Remember, it can be difficult to recognize our deceptive thoughts at first. We have to become consciously aware of our negative self-talk and the interpretations we are making. Because much of the thinking that leads to panic is instantaneous, I had to teach Sandy to slow down her thinking and calm herself physically. Like most people, Sandy had failed in past attempts to get her anxiety under wraps because she had tried to master the skills necessary to do so *after* the adversity had passed instead of *when* she first noticed her hyperarousal.

Breaking the Bad

The great news for Sandy, and for any of us who struggle with anxiety or panic, is that at any point in this fear-driven cycle we can intervene with some concrete tools to help calm ourselves down. (We'll discuss these in a later chapter.) But the skills necessary for change need to be incorporated *during* the adversity. As someone who has struggled with panic disorder, I know firsthand how terrifying and immobilizing an attack can be. I also know that the tools I learned to change my toxic thinking worked. That's what I taught Sandy, and it set her free.

Sandy seemed to get stuck with the third phase of this cycle— the cognitive distortions of *magnifying* and *catastrophizing*. When the feelings hit, her thoughts went on overdrive, no matter how hard she tried to fight them. I encouraged her not to try. That's right. I told her to stop using all her extra energy to fight the sensations and the thoughts, and to let them come. This took a great deal of trust in me as her therapist, but I had shared with Sandy about my own struggle with panic, and like me, once she realized the sensations weren't going to kill her, it was easier for her not to overreact.

Sandy was learning to stop interpreting her symptoms as dangerous and catastrophic because she began trusting that they would pass. The average length of a panic attack is ten minutes, but it can take up to thirty minutes to recover.[1] Sandy's attacks went for about five minutes, so she felt some measure of veracity in the stats I shared with her. This eased her fears.

Whether you're dealing with an anxiety disorder or with toxic thinking caused by anything else, you have to learn to be comfortable being uncomfortable. Don't avoid the symptoms. Running from them affirms your belief that you can't handle it; and you can!

So what's the key to begin this de-catastrophizing process? How do we break the bad and relentless cycle of a toxic thought-life? By using the Four Rs:

- **Recognize**
- **Refute**
- **Reframe**
- **Rewire**

The first thing I taught Sandy was to *notice* her symptoms of hyperarousal *before* they escalated. In other words, you have to **R**—*Recognize* the symptoms and make the mind-body connection before it turns into full-blown panic. To help her do this, I had Sandy list what bodily symptoms she became aware of as she felt the anxiety and panic begin to rise. (I taught her to note her physiological symptoms by doing a body scan whenever she felt an attack coming on during one week.)

This is the insight phase, but insight alone is not enough. Sandy needed to understand how to bring her catastrophic thoughts and beliefs into conscious awareness because they were driving her emotional distress. Remember, only the thoughts we accept as true and place our confidence in become our beliefs, and our actions will always follow our beliefs. If I believe I'm going to totally flip out, I will act accordingly. Sandy had to recognize that what she was telling herself was contributing to activate her alarm system.

All of us gather data from the world around us as well as from our own personal biases. We then draw conclusions that we believe are accurate. As we've seen, our interpretation of these events isn't always correct. In order to challenge or refute the aggregate data we have automatically accepted as true, we must hold it up to scrutiny.

That's where **R** number two comes in—*Refute* the veracity of what our toxic thoughts are telling us. To do this, I taught Sandy several questions to ask herself:

- What evidence do I have to support this belief?
- What evidence may there be to refute this belief?
- Could there be an alternative explanation for what's going on?
- What is the worst thing that could happen as a result of this?
- If the worst thing happened, how could I handle it, given my strengths, resources, and capacity for resilience?

Let's see how this played out for her when we pulled it apart and considered alternative explanations. By now, Sandy realized that the negative self-talk she was doing on the front end of a given situation was contributing to the problem. All her negative attributions about her symptoms were just not true. So together we wrote down some truths for her to focus on.

1. My feelings of dizziness will not cause me to faint, because fainting typically occurs when blood pressure drops. When I'm anxious, it means my blood pressure is elevated due to an increase in adrenaline and sympathetic nervous system arousal.

2. The pressure in my chest and the shortness of breath are because the muscles in my chest are constricting due to

hyperarousal. These muscles can't constrict to the point of allowing me to suffocate, no matter how unpleasant it feels. My hyperarousal is also causing me to unconsciously change my breathing patterns from normal to short breaths, and even to holding my breath. All this is tensing my muscles and not allowing the right amount of oxygen in my bloodstream.

3. Even though I feel as if I'm going crazy from the symptoms, it's just not possible. Going crazy has nothing to do with a panic attack. Besides, my body is way more resilient than I believe.

Now Sandy had information rooted in truth to counteract the fears she was experiencing. Later in the counseling process, we added a forth **R** that helped Sandy zero in on concrete biblical truths (more on that later).

Executing the Reframe

Now it was time to get Sandy to work on the third **R**—*Reframe* her negative self-talk statements into positive ones. On a blank piece of paper, I had her write her negative thoughts and record the situation that caused her to think them. Negative self-talk statements are generally our beliefs. Next, she was to record how these statements made her feel about herself or anyone else involved. Finally, we worked on coming up with some positive counterstatements to refute each of her toxic thoughts. Here are some examples of what I did with Sandy:

Situation: I heard my coworker saying some mean things to my boss about my performance.

Recognize negative self-talk statement: I'm a total failure at my job. I'll probably get fired. I'll never get another good job.

Feelings: Angry, disappointed, confused, hurt.

Refuting statements: Could there be an alternative explanation for my coworker's comments?

What would I tell a friend in this situation?

What evidence do I have to support the belief that I'll get fired?

If the worst thing happens, how could I handle it?

Reframe positive counterstatements:
Maybe my coworker was dealing with her own insecurities about the project.

I would encourage a friend to confront the coworker in love and speak to the boss about the situation.

I have no real evidence that I will be fired.

If I did get fired, I could look for another job. I really am good at what I do, and I've demonstrated resiliency in my professional and personal life on many occasions.

Sandy's anxiety was driven by fear, something we all struggle with from time to time, even if we don't have an anxiety disorder. She underestimated her ability to cope with the difficulties of life, and she overestimated the negative outcomes. Sandy is a very capable and intelligent woman. She has held several prior positions in the corporate world that were impressive, but because of her anxiety disorder and her catastrophic thinking, she generally underestimated her abilities. I wanted her to consider these ideas as she developed her counterstatements. As you can see, Sandy's statements reflected the concept of resiliency.

I had Sandy add one more heading to her list of counterstatements:

Possible Coping Strategies. This would give her an opportunity to problem-solve and use her executive learning skills. The problem with toxic thinking is that we are generally predicting negative outcomes to any given situation that is causing us distress. Instead of staying stuck, we have to create movement. Movement is simply a call to action. Here is the situation I have. Here are the choices I have to deal with it. Remember, only you can be part of the solution. Only you get to choose what action you will take.

When we get stuck in predicting outcomes, we have to generate some possibility thinking. The Possible Coping Strategy idea will help you use your strengths and develop resiliency instead of focusing on catastrophic and negative outcomes. For Sandy, it looked like this:

- I could confront my team member about what I overheard her saying.
- I can have a conversation with my boss and explain my concerns and those of my team.
- If for some reason I were to get fired, I could apply for other jobs. I have lots of connections, and I know lots of people in the industry who respect me.
- If that didn't work out, I could pursue another career field. I have always been interested in marketing.

After we went through this part of the exercise, Sandy not only felt better, but she was able to see how to switch lenses and use her resources and strengths to brainstorm solid possibilities for worst-case scenarios. In the end, Sandy didn't lose her job. In fact, her coworker apologized, and her boss defended her. She was able to use this situation to see how her catastrophic thinking got her off-track. She was able to recognize just how much energy she wasted on things that never came about.

The last **R** in the list for Sandy to consider was for *Rewire*. To rewire neuropathways, we have to start by taking those crazy thoughts captive. It all begins with *acceptance.* You have to accept what your body is doing when it feels out of control. That means going with the flow and not tensing up, not fighting the sensations, just letting them happen. If you can do this on the front end, the surge of the adrenaline causing the panic will metabolize and be reabsorbed in a shorter period of time. For the rewiring process to occur, we have to retrain our brains by setting our minds.

Setting the mind requires that we have something to set it on besides the lies and toxic thoughts. If we don't set our minds, they will be set for us. This is the time to write out, meditate on, and repeatedly focus on some positive counterstatements. You may have to do this over and over during the day. Practice telling yourself these truths every time you are tempted to think negatively. The more you practice, the more you will establish new neuropathways. Let's see how to get started with this.

Countering Lies with Truth

The idea of positive thinking has been around for a long time, at least since 1952 when Norman Vincent Peale wrote *The Power of Positive Thinking*. It sold five million copies and remained on the *New York Times* Bestseller list for years. It's obvious that for a long time people have been interested in changing their thinking patterns, but not everyone succeeds.

Why do some people change and others don't? Because we get attached to our negative self-talk! As crazy as that sounds, it feels normal for us. It's a difficult habit to break, and it's hard to give up our "set-in-stone beliefs." Perhaps most important is that many of us lack the skillset for developing resiliency, and only resilient people are willing to change and take risks. They welcome change and personal growth.

If you're willing to try to develop some new habits and rewire your brain, let's do it! I've given you lots of questions so far to challenge the negative attributions we are all prone to make, but one thing remains to be addressed. You must have *some* level of belief in the veracity of the counterstatements you develop. It won't work if the statements you use to counter your negative attributions hold no truth for you.

So here are some tips for you when writing your counterstatements:

- Don't use negative phrases when doing your counterstatements. For example, don't say, "I'm not going to panic when I give my speech." Instead, try saying, "I'm confident and prepared for this presentation, and I will do my best; that's all I can do." Use resilience-based self-talk. Telling yourself something bad won't happen can amp up your anxiety.

- Try keeping the reframes in the here-and-now—while something is happening. For example, "I'm in control of this panic right now." Most of our negative self-talk happens in the moment, so our counters need to be focused on the present tense as well. If you can't stay in the moment, begin the reframe like this: "I am willing to . . . experience anxiety, because I know it will pass." "I can cope . . . with this anxiety, because I have done it in the past."

- Again, your counterstatements must hold some personal credibility in your mind to be effective.

How To Rewire

The Power of Neural Circuitry

When the apostle Paul told us to "take every thought captive," he wasn't kidding. Inspired by God to pen those words, Paul must have known that our Creator hardwired damaging thoughts to change our neural circuitry for the worse. Dr. Jennings also weighs in on how our thoughts rewire our brains:

> Brain Derived Neurotrophic Factor (BDNF) is a protein acting like fertilizer for our brain cells. . . . BDNF doesn't leave the DNA as BDNF but as a precursor protein called proBDNF. But proBDNF is not inactive. In fact, its effects are opposite BDNF. While BDNF is fertilizer for neurons, proBDNF is like weed killer to neurons. If proBDNF binds to dendrites, axons, or neurons, it will kill them. The critical issue to determine whether a neuron or neural circuit gets BDNF (fertilizer) or proBDNF (weed killer) is the presence of an enzyme that cleaves or cuts the longer chain molecule (proBDNF) into the shorter molecule BDNF. If the enzyme is present, BDNF is available and the circuit grows stronger. If the enzyme is not present, proBDNF is not cleaved and thus proBDNF prunes the circuit back.[2]

What does all this mean for us? How can thinking positive thoughts actually wire our brains even if we aren't doing anything behaviorally to act out and experience what we are telling ourselves? The more we use our neural circuits, the more they fire and the stronger they become. If the circuits remain idle, they don't produce the enzymes necessary to grow, and in time the circuit can atrophy.

Let me explain, again using Sandy as an example. We know Sandy had engaged in catastrophic thinking about her job, her teammates, her boss, and getting fired. Once she recognized her negative thinking, she could now decide to take every thought captive and reframe her thoughts. But once she actually started *practicing* telling herself the truth, she began producing in her brain the enzyme that, if present, turns the proBDNF into BDNF. That's what gets her circuits firing, recruiting more neurons and making new connections. Repetition is what makes everything get stronger. There is no other way around it. Practice makes perfect.

If you don't believe it, think about what it takes to learn a new language. Maybe you've heard that one of the best brain builders is to learn a foreign language when you get older. Why is that? Because studies have shown that learning new words causes new synaptic connections to form. Every day you practice causes more firing and more connections. Guess what enzyme this produces in the brain? Yep, the one necessary to cleave proBDNF into BDNF.

Let's say you learn Spanish because you move to Mexico for two years. You work hard to learn the language, and everyday you're making a valiant attempt to speak it. Then you move back to Virginia where you are originally from, and you have no real reason to speak Spanish. Five years go by, and now no circuits are firing anymore on the Spanish front. What happens to your ability to speak the language? The enzyme that cleaves to proBDNF isn't being produced anymore, is it? So slowly but surely your neural circuitry for the language is diminished.

Now in this example you can see how a person's thoughts are being acted out behaviorally. You think about learning the language, and you actually have conversations with others using it. But what if you never did anything behaviorally? Would the synapses still fire? In other words, if Sandy only thought about having a conversation with her team about their performance, if she only thought about working on her relationship with her boss, if she only thought about the possibilities of a new career, would that still change the neuro-networks in her brain?

The answer is yes! Dr. Jennings explains that in the year 2000,

Karl Herholz and Wolf-Dieter Heiss discovered that stroke patients who merely imagined moving an affected limb actually activated the corresponding motor circuits in their brains. This is the concept of visualization in artistic and athletic performance: brain studies have shown that when musicians imagine playing a piece of music, the same motor pathways activate as if they were actually playing their instrument, even though no muscles are being moved. *The thoughts we think actually reshape our brains!*[3] (italics mine)

All of this should be enough evidence to convince you that what you tell yourself is everything. Think about what you love. Think about what you're good at. You didn't get good at things you didn't practice, whether it's your work, your sport, or your hobby. You put in the time to practice, and it paid off with success if you kept at it. The same goes for your thought-life. You put garbage in, garbage is going to come out. You put in what is pure, lovely, and of good report, and that's what you'll get. Peace. Contentment. Health. Well-being. Isn't that worth it!

NOTES

[1] Ron Alexander, "Chronicle," *New York Times,* May 31, 1994, http://www.nytimes.com/1994/05/31/nyregion/chronicle-254657.html.

[2] Jennings, *The God Shaped Brain.*

[3] Jennings, *The God Shaped Brain.*

Chapter Five

DEADLY DETOURS: THE POWER OF COGNITIVE DISTORTIONS

Above all else, guard your heart,
for everything you do flows from it.

—Proverbs 4:23

Finally, brothers and sisters, whatever is true, whatever is noble,
whatever is right, whatever is pure, whatever is lovely,
whatever is admirable—if anything is excellent or praiseworthy—
think about such things.

—Philippians 4:8

Dr. Albert Ellis and Dr. Aaron Beck were pioneers in the field of psychology. Beck developed what is known today as Cognitive Behavior Therapy (CBT) and Ellis gave us Rational Emotive Behavioral Therapy (REBT). Both men were highly interested in how to help patients change their thinking to overcome depression and anxiety, because they recognized the impact that thinking had on our emotional and physical well-being.

This relationship between thoughts and beliefs has long been a topic of discussion. Some two thousand years ago, a philosopher named Epictetus had this to say about the power of our thoughts: "What disturbs men's minds is not events but their judgements on events." This gives credibility to the idea that it's the *meaning* (the interpretation) we attach to the circumstances and events in our lives that causes our emotional distress.

Ellis developed what he coined as an **ABC** model to help patients understand how this chain of events occurs. In his model, A stands for an *activating event* or the *adversity* that caused an upset in feelings, B stands for the *belief(s)* that ran through your mind when you were confronted with the activating event, and C stands for the *consequence*, or the behavior(s) that resulted from the belief. In other words, what you did in response to the thoughts and feelings the situation created.

People's belief systems were important to Beck and Ellis because they believed people created their own misery by what they were *continually* telling themselves. Their thoughts, beliefs, and the resulting consequences of their thinking were not allowing them to regulate their emotions in an adaptive way. Unproductive patterns needed to be altered for optimum health and emotional well-being to occur.

Take a minute to assess how *you* react to stress, setbacks, challenges, or new experiences. Do you navigate through them well? Do you find it difficult to rid yourself of negative emotions? Do you have very few positive emotions? Do you fear stepping outside the box? Do you attempt to problem solve, or do you just emote? Are you flexible in your thinking? Are your beliefs set in stone?

Ellis believed that we upset ourselves by holding *inflexible beliefs*. This is key, because without some flexibility in our belief systems, we are destined to stay stuck in the same maladaptive patterns of thinking. That's why I like to call them "set-in-stone beliefs." They are like set concrete in our minds. The great news about the set-in-stone beliefs we hold is that they can be changed or modified.

How to Switch Off Toxic Thoughts

So far we've learned that toxic thinking appears on our radar screen pretty automatically. Toxic thinking is a trap, a deadly detour from resilience and well-being, so we have to notice and be aware of it. I know by now you probably are sick of my belaboring this point, but I cannot emphasize this enough. I trust that after you're done reading this book, the one thing you will surely take away from it is learning to be a noticer!

We can use the acronyms **TRAP** and **STOP** to help keep on the alert for negative self-talk. **TRAP** will help you notice your current thought patterns, and **STOP** will help you move toward change. Here is an example of how it all begins: we have loads of negative self-defeating thoughts that come at us all day. If you're old enough, you will know what ticker tape is (a ticker tape is a paper strip on which messages were recorded in a telegraphic tape machine), so you can follow my metaphor here.

Used ticker tape was diced into confetti and thrown from the windows above parades. They were even labeled "ticker tape parades." If you've ever seen one in New York, you know it looks as if it was snowing because of all the ticker tape confetti in the air. This ticker tape confetti is a good visual representation of our thoughts and the messages they carry with them.

These messages can be relentless. We generally respond to them by replaying them over and over in our minds (that's called ruminating). The more we think about them, the more we buy into them and *believe* them. Once a thought becomes a belief, we place our confidence in it as a *fact*. Once we do that, we give it power. When it has power, it controls our behavior. We saw in the last chapter how constant repetition of thoughts affects our neural circuitry. Here is what you need to become aware of with the **TRAP** acronym:

T—Think toxic thoughts
R—Replay toxic thoughts
A—Assume toxic thoughts are true
P—give Power to toxic thoughts

The way to combat these automatic thoughts is to slow down our thinking (we learned this in Chapter One). I know this is hard, but this is the first key step. Because these thoughts are so automatic, we don't often realize that they are gaining momentum and that they will eventually sabotage us if we allow it. The question isn't what *if* the thoughts come, it's what do I do *when* they come? By now you should be well aware of the answer to this question: notice. Slow down. Take thoughts captive on the front end, just as the Bible teaches.

Once you slow down, take a minute to test the truth of the thought. Use Socratic questioning to test it. Ask yourself if there is any evidence to support your belief in the veracity of the thought. This can be hard, because sometimes there may be some evidence that the thought is true. For example, let's say I get in a fight with my spouse. The way my spouse copes when we are in an argument is by shutting down emotionally and not talking. This triggers memories of my mother who would get angry with me, say mean things, and then withdraw love. So, when my spouse shuts down on me, the ticker tapes that play in my head say the following:

1. You're a loser.
2. You aren't lovable.
3. You're a failure at relationships.
4. Your spouse is going to leave you.

Let's break this down. When the thoughts come, slow . . . them . . . down. If you learn to do this with thought number one, you can stop this ticker tape chain before you get all the way down to telling yourself your spouse is going to leave you. You can test the thought, check yourself for thinking errors, and oppose the initial thought that you're a loser (remember our Four R's—Recognize, Refute, Reframe, Rewire). Now use the STOP acronym to do this.

S—Slow it down

T—Test the thought

O—Oppose the thought and Offer up evidence to refute it

P—Practice healthier ways of thinking every day

After we notice the patterns and triggers for our toxic thoughts, we need to learn to slow down our thinking by pausing. This takes practice, because we are so used to doing everything *fast*. If thoughts are coming at us to the tune of seventy thousand per day, this means we have to do a lot of slowing down in order to practice our thought-stopping. How do we do it? How do we really slow down our thoughts after we notice them? We quiet ourselves by sitting, closing our eyes, focusing on our breathing, and clearing the mind of all distractions.

Once we're calm, we can then begin testing the thoughts and identifying the cognitive distortions we may be making. Identifying the thinking errors requires that we commit them to memory and zero in on the ones that we tend to do the most (the list will be provided in the next section). That way we can notice better.

By now you may be saying, "That's great, Rita, but how am I supposed to do this at work or on an insane day with my kids screaming?" You improvise. That's what you do. If you're at work, take five minutes and go to the bathroom. If you're at home with the kids, take five minutes and go hide in the bathroom! Perhaps you can jot down a few of your racing thoughts and beliefs and save them for a later time when things quiet down. Then you can go through the process of testing the thoughts and replacing them.

THINK THIS NOT THAT

The key is don't give up. If we can land a man on the moon, we can figure out a way to be intentional about this work. Push through. Persevere. Practice.

The Big Eight

We all make plenty of thinking errors and deceptive thoughts on a daily basis. Some of them have already been mentioned, but in this section I want to provide you with a concrete list and descriptive analysis of what I call the Big Eight Thinking Errors all of us are prone to make. Read these carefully and take note of the ones you find yourself doing the most. Commit them to memory so that you will notice when you're doing them.

1. Should, Must, Ought To Be, and Have To Be Statements

To begin, let's take a look at what Dr. Ellis believed to be at the core of all our irrational beliefs in one form or another: the should, must, ought-to-be / have-to-be statements. For example:

- I *should be* perfect.
- Other people *must* treat me fairly.
- I *must have* a good _____ (fill in blank: body, job, kids, spouse).
- I *must* perform well or I'm worthless.
- I *have to have* others' acceptance.
- Life *ought to be* less painful.

Beliefs like these are inflexible, and they can easily lead to anxiety, depression, self-pity, anger, and guilt. The goal here is to help you learn to morph beliefs that you have set in stone into less demanding schemas. This leads to a healthier lifestyle. For example, part of Sandy's problem was that she held many of the inflexible beliefs above that kept her stuck. Here are a few we uncovered in our work together:

- She *had to be* perfect.
- Her boss *ought to* treat her fairly.
- She *had to* perform well because her value and worth were tied into having a successful career.

As we talked, I helped her challenge these beliefs with the following questions:

- Why must others treat me fairly?
- What happens if they don't?
- Why must I have acceptance from others?
- What happens for me if others don't accept me?

Matthew McKay and Patrick Fanning suggest four ways we can determine when these "should" statements reflect an unhealthy, versus a healthy, lifestyle.

- Is the statement flexible? Does it allow for exceptions?
- Is the statement based on your own experience, or have you adopted it from someone else?
- Is the statement realistic and does it take into account all possible consequences?
- Does the statement help you reach your goals, solve your problems, and meet your needs?[2]

After exploring each of the aforementioned statements, Sandy realized her "set-in-stone" beliefs were unrealistic and were keeping her from reaching her life goals. She also started to see that at the core of all her beliefs was a fear of rejection, insecurity, and feelings of being devalued (remember our discussion on needs). I proposed that although it is not pleasant to have other people treat you unfairly, find you unacceptable, or not like you, it isn't going to ruin your life. Sandy needed something bigger to place her confidence in for value and worth. Enter Jesus.

The truth is that God accepts Sandy (as he does you and me) just as she is, and he loves her immeasurably more than she can imagine. That's in stone. That is truth. As long as she can appropriate that into her belief system, she can afford to have a few people not like her. When we place our source of value in anything other than Christ, it's always up for grabs. We have to keep performing to get those needs met, and that can get seriously tiresome.

"It's painful, though," Sandy retorted! "Yes, it is," I said, "But remember; we *can* learn to be comfortable while we are uncomfortable. No one said life was fair. No one said relationships would be easy. It's part of the fallen world we live in. The real question is how will we respond to these difficult stressors in our lives? Acceptance is the key."

2. Jumping to Conclusions / Mind Reading / Fortune Telling

The next biggie on the cognitive distortion list is jumping to conclusions. This cognitive distortion has two partners in crime: mind reading and fortune telling. It looked like this for Sandy. She told me, "I was sitting in my office and I heard my boss using my name several times while he was talking with a client on the phone. This client was particularly difficult, and I knew he wouldn't have anything good to say about me. After their conversation was over, my boss called me into his office. I braced myself for the fallout!"

Let's take a look at Sandy's interpretations. Just like Epictetus said, Sandy's problem was that she attached a false interpretation to the phone call from what she assumed was a disgruntled client. This caused Sandy anxiety. She automatically concluded without any evidence that her client was complaining about her to the boss. She was mind reading. Sandy had no evidence to support that belief (except that *she* felt the client was difficult). Furthermore, she jumped to conclusions that her boss was going to chew her out because of the phone call. Sandy was fortune telling. She automatically assumed things would turn out badly and that her predictions were an already established fact (without even hearing what her boss had to say).

Sandy was quite surprised to learn that the client had called to praise her for her professionalism and told her boss he was impressed with her capabilities and her patience because he knew he had been difficult at times. Her boss called her into his office to commend her!

3. Overgeneralization

Overgeneralization is next on our list of thinking errors. This is when we assume that just because we've had one bad experience with a person, place, or thing, it will *always* be repeated. For example, because Sandy had some run-ins with her boss, she assumed (falsely) that *all* their interactions would be difficult. Sandy also believed that because a colleague at work made a critical remark about her performance, *everyone* must believe she is a failure at her job.

Overgeneralizing can take many forms. If a spouse or a friend has betrayed you, you may automatically assume that all men/ women are untrustworthy. If your internal monologues include words like "never, always, or everyone," you're overgeneralizing.

4. Personalization

Sandy had another problem with her thinking that we uncovered once we talked about overgeneralizing. It's called personalization. Personalization is the tendency to attribute problems to your own doing. If you and your spouse have an argument, you believe that it's because of something *you* did or said. You don't take into account the other person's contribution to the problem or situation.

When we personalize, we miss out on the causes of the problem that we *did not* create. The other problem with personalization is that it lowers resiliency. If I do poorly on an exam and I immediately berate myself and impugn my character, saying, "I got a D because I'm an idiot," and I'm suggesting that "idiot" is who *I am*, it's unchangeable. The truth is, I can make a choice to study harder, and that could change the outcome of my grade next time I take an exam. When I set my character up as the problem, I'm basically saying that I was born an idiot and I'm going to stay an idiot, no matter what I do. Pay attention to those thoughts.

Sandy's interpretation about the remark of her colleague confirmed her already established belief that she was a failure at her job (personalizers only look at themselves). She didn't consider that her colleague could have contributed to the problem.

The truth was that Sandy's coworker made several mistakes on a project they were working on together and took no responsibility. Because Sandy was personalizing, she missed the causes of the problem that were not her fault. Internalizing personalizers see the cause of a problem as being something intrinsically wrong with themselves: they are somehow flawed. Externalizing personalizers attribute all the problems to others' behavior and seldom look at their own stuff. Either tendency lowers the capacity for resiliency.

I helped Sandy to see that when we believe the cause of the problem is related to our behavior, we have the power (resilience) to change. But we have to change the core beliefs that drive the behavior. When we constantly impugn our character by making toxic statements such as "I didn't get a good performance review on the project because I'm a failure," we stay stuck. The belief that I'm a failure requires deeper work to change or modify the set-in-stone belief.

5. Disqualifying the Positive

Disqualifying the positive is a way we overestimate a negative outcome and minimize our ability to cope with difficult situations. We reject our positive experiences, or our strengths, and we focus instead on the negative aspects of our situation or our character. In this way, we fail to acknowledge our capacity for resiliency if something negative does occur.

The truth is that people are far more resilient than we think. If you don't believe it, take a look at some of the terrible calamities that have occurred over the last decades and how people have rebuilt their lives, their fortunes, and their cities and towns.

- Look at how the people of New York rallied after 9/11. They rebuilt with great resolve and courage.
- In December 2004, a great tsunami hit in Sri Lanka, Indonesia, Thailand, India, Bangladesh, Myanmar, Maldives, and Malaysia and killed two hundred twenty thousand people.
- In 2010, an earthquake in Haiti destroyed even more people.
- Hurricane Katrina. Remember her damage?
- Think of the heroic people who withstood Nazi prison camps.

We will never know what we are capable of until we actually face something profoundly difficult. When we disqualify the positive, we cut our legs out from under ourselves before we begin to brainstorm possibilities for moving forward.

6. Catastrophizing

Catastrophizing is the number-one anxiety provoker. It's blowing things way out of proportion. For example, your child gets a

D in his fifth-grade English class, and you conclude he will never amount to anything. When something bad happens to us, our self-talk plays a familiar tape that says, "I can't handle this." We self-sabotage with "what if" statements like these:

- What if I lose my job?
- What if I don't get married?
- What if my spouse cheats?
- What if I don't get the promotion?
- What if I don't get into the best school?
- What if I don't get pregnant?
- What if I don't lose weight?

What if statements kill our capacity for resiliency by undermining our beliefs about our strengths. I taught Sandy to ask herself: "If the worst-case scenario did occur, is it true that I couldn't handle it?" This is where brainstorming possible solutions comes in. Magnifying and catastrophizing do one toxic thing very well: they convince you to underestimate your ability to cope.

The key is to identify your strengths and look for past situations where you used them to cope. For example, people who struggle with anxiety such as panic disorder are prone to catastrophic thinking. Consider this scenario:

Katie was terrified of having a panic attack in the grocery store. She had experienced several episodes there and avoided the place like the plague. Her belief system told her that she would faint, or freak out and make a fool of herself. Here are some possible reframes for Katie that would help her to see things differently. Using our **STOP** acronym, she could

S—Slow it down. Hit the pause button.
If I did have a panic attack again at the store, I could cope by deep breathing.

T—Test the thought.

How likely is it that I will really faint? Freak out? Be carried away in a straight-jacket? My therapist said that anxiety ramps up my nervous system, so fainting is highly unlikely.

O—Oppose the thought.

Even if something did happen in the store, I don't have to be embarrassed. What is the likelihood I'll ever see those people again?

P—Practice healthier ways of thinking every day.

If I felt like I was going to faint, I could ask someone for help. Truthfully, it's much more likely that people would express concern if they saw me in distress.

Once Katie started practicing these new techniques every time a situation occurred, she soon noticed she began to gain mastery over them. It just took a little time and effort.

7. Emotional Reasoning

Emotional Reasoning is one of the more dangerous thinking errors because it assaults our sense of self. Here, we assume our negative feelings are a reflection of how things really are. We feel embarrassed or inadequate, so we believe we are intrinsically flawed. "I feel inadequate; therefore I *am* inadequate." This flies in the face of everything God says about his kids. "For God so loved the world that he gave his one and only Son, that whoever believes in him shall not perish but have eternal life" (John 3:16). If this is true, and as Christians we profess to believe it, then we are worth everything!

Sandy's childhood contributed a great deal to her distortion of emotional reasoning. Her parents had divorced when she was ten, and her father had been quite the critic. His negative comments to Sandy and her mom hurt her deeply. Things like, "You can't do anything right, you'll never amount to a hill of beans," and "if it can be messed up, you'll find a way to do it," all served to make Sandy feel very inadequate. Because she felt that way, she began to believe she was intrinsically flawed.

8. All-or-Nothing Thinking

This led Sandy to the final cognitive distortion we'll discuss here: all-or-nothing thinking. Because Sandy felt so inadequate, she decided that she had to make up for it by being perfect in her performance (all this was happening beneath the conscious surface of awareness). There was no middle ground for her; she was either perfect, or she was a total failure. I explained to her that between those two opposing beliefs lay a lot of middle ground. Her challenge was to train her brain, modify her belief system, and move to a more middle-ground area.

We talked about Sandy considering the idea that she wasn't perfect, and neither was anyone else. She, like all of us, would sometimes make mistakes, but those mistakes did not provide substantial evidence that she was a failure in life. Neither did her father's words. It took Sandy time, patience, and a lot of practice to get down these principles for change, but once she did she was on a roll. There was no turning back to the past and its dysfunctional ways.

These eight cognitive distortions aren't the end of the story. They are simply the top contenders I see in my therapeutic practice. I would, however, be remiss in not including some of the other common thinking errors for consideration. Below you will find additional cognitive distortions, along with their explanations, to be on the watch for.

Externalizing—The opposite of personalizing is externalizing. Folks who do this take a very objective point of view when it comes to life, relationships, and problematic situations; they blame everyone else. Nothing is their fault. They may not feel guilt or regret, but they do generally feel angry with everyone else for not toeing the line.

Magnifying/Minimizing—Magnifying sits on the front end of catastrophizing. You might say it's making a mountain out of a molehill. If we don't stop the string of ticker tape thoughts coming into our minds, things seem to go haywire, and before you know it, we're in full-blown catastrophe mode. The opposite of magnifying is *minimizing*. Here, you shrink the importance of things, such as your feelings when you're hurt, saying they don't really matter, for one reason or the other. This is often known as the martyr complex. Comparing yourself or what you're going through with what someone else is feeling is another way to open the door for minimizing. It's healthy to feel your feelings when you have them. Minimizing does your pain a disservice.

Self-Defeating Thinking—This one is a broad, generalized category of deceptive thought patterns that lead you one place—down the drain. It boils down to rumination. These are patterns of thinking that keep us from getting what we want or from reaching our goals. Ask yourself if there is an alternative way to view your problem or situation, a way that would get what you want and help you to reach your goals.

Is There a Reason We Fall into Thinking Traps?

Yes! At the heart of thinking errors is something that Karen Reivich and Andrew Shatté call *induction*, the process by which we build general rules from an accumulation of specific examples. Inductive reasoning makes broad generalizations from specific observations. With inductive inference, we go from specifics to generalities. Take a look: I encounter a (specific) dog. He bites me. I conclude all dogs (general) are dangerous, so I must stay away from dogs.[3]

I don't need to encounter *all* dogs to make this judgment; I make it because my *experience* tells me it's true. (I generalize and jump to conclusions). The truth is *all* dogs are not dangerous. Inductive reasoning leaves room for our conclusions to be wrong. It proceeds from specific premises to general conclusions. The problem comes in when we apply *inductive* reasoning to situations that require *deductive* reasoning. Deductive reasoning proceeds from general premises to a specific conclusion.[4]

What's going on in the brain when these judgments are occurring? According to Daniel Siegel, our experiences stimulate neural firing and sculpt our emerging synaptic connections. This is how experience changes the structure of the brain itself. Using the dog analogy, Siegel goes on to explain:

> If you've always had positive experiences with dogs and have enjoyed having them in your life, you may feel pleasure and excitement when a neighbor's new dog comes bounding toward you. But if you've ever been severely bitten, your neural firing patterns may instead help create a sense of dread and panic, causing your entire body to shrink away from the pooch. If on top of having had a prior bad experience with a dog you also have a shy temperament, such an encounter

may be even more fraught with fear. But whatever your experience and underlying temperament, *transformation is possible*. Learning to focus your attention in specific therapeutic ways can help you override that old coupling of fear with dogs. The intentional focus of attention is actually a form of self-directed experience. It stimulates new patterns of neural firing to create new synaptic linkages (italics mine).[5]

The good news that can't be driven home enough is that transformation is not only possible, but with intentional practice and a therapeutic skillset to work from, it is highly probable. We just have to be aware of our cognitive distortions and of how we are applying inductive reasoning where it isn't called for.

Reivich and Shatté say:

Overgeneralizing is exactly the trap we fall into when we take one of our inductive rules and apply it where it doesn't belong. We fall into thinking traps because inductive thinking is useful. We should be more aware of our shortcomings—that we may not have all the information in our reach—and we should not be so confident that we considered the problem comprehensively. Problems arise when we allocate our resources based on these mistaken judgments. Our resilience is diminished when we commit ourselves to action based on false belief.[6]

So what does all of this mean for you and me? It means we have to key into which thinking errors we are most prone to making. It means that we have to develop a skillset to recognize thinking traps. It means we have to memorize and become so familiar with the thinking errors we make that it becomes second nature to recognize when we are making one. We have to realize that using inductive reasoning to manage life and the world around us can, and often will, lead us into wrong thinking.

In the next chapter, we'll look at how to identify and challenge set-in-stone beliefs and unpack how our style of relating impacts the beliefs that may be keeping us stuck. This will equip us to move from the insight stage of noticing to the concrete stage of creating real and lasting change.

NOTES

[1]"Epictetus," *Internet Encyclopedia of Philosophy*, http://www.iep.utm.edu/epictetu/.

[2]Matthew McKay and Patrick Fanning, *Self Esteem: A Proven Program of Cognitive Techniques for Assessing, Improving & Maintaining Your Self-Esteem* (Oakland, CA: New Harbinger Publications, 2000).

[3]Karen Reivich and Andrew Shatté, *The Resilience Factor: 7 Keys to Finding Your Inner Strength and Overcoming Life's Hurdles* (New York: Three Rivers Press/Random House, 2002), 117–119.

[4]Alina Bradford, "Deductive Reasoning vs. Inductive Reasoning," *Live Science*, July 24, 2017, http://www.livescience.com/21569-deduction-vs-induction.html.

[5]Siegel, *Mindsight*, 41–42.

[6]Reivich and Shatté, 119.

PART TWO

TOXIC
TRAUMA

Chapter Six

TROUBLESHOOTING

Do not be conformed to this world, but be transformed by the renewal
of your mind, that by testing you may discern what is the will of God,
what is good and acceptable and perfect.

—Romans 12:2 ESV

Thinking is the place where intelligent actions begin.
We pause long enough to look more carefully at a situation,
to see more of its character, to think about why it's happening,
to notice how it's affecting us and others.

—Margaret J. Wheatley

Now that we're familiar with the Big Eight Thinking Errors, we are better equipped to recognize how these negative attributions are affecting our everyday behavior. In Chapter Five, we looked at Sandy's thoughts, feelings, beliefs, and the cognitive distortions she was prone to make. Now we want to focus on how the beliefs we hold on to affect us behaviorally and what the consequences of those behaviors are for our mental health. Is there really something we can do about all this? Yes!

You have to uncover why a situation causes you to feel and act the way you do if you're going to gain mastery over your thoughts and learn to modify set-in-stone beliefs. If we can identify the behavioral patterns that result from those beliefs, we can identify what is causing us to overreact and what often sabotages our decision-making process. We can then choose in the moment what the healthiest options are for us instead of feeling helpless. In other words, we can troubleshoot what needs to be done on the front end of an adversity so that we can take control of our thoughts, attitudes, actions, and beliefs.

Let's go back to Sandy. In the last chapter, we discovered that one of her set-in-stone beliefs was that she felt like a failure at her job. But let's dig deeper. What did that *mean* for Sandy? How did she define "failure," and what did it say about her intrinsic worth if she was a failure? Making sense of her narrative would help Sandy better understand the impact her story had on the coping strategies she used to navigate through life. Sandy's husband told her it was her boss who was the problem, but Sandy had a hard time believing this. Her boss was very well respected in the business world, and given his position and reputation, she couldn't imagine that he could be the problem. It must be her.

As we talked further about it, Sandy revealed that in her family of origin, doing a good job and being reliable and responsible meant everything. You had to be an achiever because Dad was a very successful businessman. Failure meant anything less than perfection. Sandy told me she craved his approval. Because he was emotionally distant, he didn't dole out praises very often.

I asked Sandy to be curious about what this meant for her. She said that because she never heard praise from her father, she felt uncertain about his love and approval of her outside of her performance. The tension this created for her made her try harder to gain what she so desperately needed from him. A crystalizing moment occurred for her when she realized that this was exactly what she was doing with her boss.

In Sandy's family, if you were successful it meant you were valuable. If you were valuable, this meant that you would be highly respected. In Sandy's eyes, if she was a failure at her job, if her boss didn't praise her, it meant she wasn't valued or respected. In addition, her coworkers would see her as inadequate. We had to get busy troubleshooting these beliefs.

Challenging Set-in-Stone Beliefs

If you are going to learn to avoid thinking traps, change your set-in-stone beliefs, and rewire your brain in the process, you have to pay close attention to what you believe about effecting change in your own life. Any doubts you have about your ability to change your behavior will limit how much any of these skills will help you. So pay attention to your self-talk. Do this by listening to what you tell yourself about learning something new, taking a risk, or changing a behavior. If you believe change is just too hard for you, that you can't do it, or that you always start something only to give up, you're probably going to stay stuck.

When we're examining our beliefs, we have to ask ourselves if we're focusing on what Reivich and Shatté call *"why"* or *"what-next"* beliefs.[1] *Why beliefs* relate directly to the cause of the problem or adversity we're facing. In other words, *why beliefs* provide the answer to why we think a situation or problem occurred. Sandy's belief that she wasn't good at managing people was the answer to *why* she didn't get a desired promotion ("I didn't get the job promotion because my boss thinks I am not good enough at managing people").

What-next beliefs reflect a fear of how things will play out in the future. People who hold these beliefs feel like their predictions about future events are an already established fact and will affect everything they do as they move forward in life (remember, this is fortune telling). Sandy's *what-next beliefs* looked like this:

- Loosing this promotion will hurt any future career moves I will make.

- I'll never advance in this company or in any other one for that matter.
- I just didn't click with my boss because I'm incapable of a good working relationship with a man.

If we're going to learn how to troubleshoot, we have to look at our *why beliefs* and see how much they are actually contributing to our problem. Keep in mind that not all the factors that contribute to our problems can be changed, or even fixed. The key is finding the piece, or pieces, we can have some measure of control over.

Sandy may think, for example, that she has little chance of changing her boss's mind about her ability to manage people effectively. That could be true. She can't control what her boss thinks, feels, or believes. Instead, she can choose to focus on learning how to build strong, healthy relationships with male authority figures. That's a goal within her control.

Whatever piece of the problem seems most amenable to change is where you want to start problem solving. Remember that when we are facing an adversity, our prefrontal cortex (logic and reason) gets bypassed as our limbic brain (emotion) revs up, so in order to not act impulsively we have to slow down the thought process and use our skills to learn to calm ourselves.

Finding Your Style

Our initial assessment of our problem will determine the trajectory we take with our troubleshooting skills. Sandy, like all of us, developed a style of explaining the events that affects the way she perceives the problems she faces and the cognitive distortions she is prone to make.

Reivich and Shatté talk about how our explanatory styles influence our response to adversity. They suggest the following explanatory styles: *me-not-me, always-not-always, everything-not-everything.*[2]

If you're a subjective person you're going to view your problems through the lens of the "me" style (remember personalization). This means that when there's a problem, or an adversity, you tend to look at something *you* have done as the cause of it. If your boyfriend doesn't call, it's because *you* have done something wrong. If the kids aren't doing well, it's because *you* haven't been a good enough mom. If your husband cheated, it's because *you* weren't a good enough wife. All these examples focus on *self* as the problem.

The opposite explanatory style is being "other" focused. Other-focused people are objective. They think every problem or situation is about someone else's behavior, or something someone else did wrong. This is the "not me" style. "He's a loser; that's why he cheated." "My son is lazy; that's why he isn't doing well in school." "My boyfriend doesn't call because he's selfish with his time."

Sandy's set-in-stone belief that she would never advance in her company, or in any other company, reveals another characteristic of our processing mentality that Reivich and Shatté call, "always versus not always."[3] Sandy generalizes that she will *never* be promoted no matter where she works. The betrayed wife with an *always* style might think, "I'll never make my husband happy." When Sandy had a disagreement with her boss, what was her immediate reaction? Her "always" style led her to think, "My boss is always right; I guess I'm not too good at my job." The *not always* style is just the opposite. To expand her view, Sandy might reason, "I may not always get things right, but I'm pretty darn good at my job."

The final explanatory style that Reivich and Shatté mention is "everything versus not everything."[4] This means, to what degree do you believe that the cause of the problem or adversity will affect "everything or not everything" in your life? When you survey your set-in-stone beliefs, do they suggest that your home life, your work life, your social life, and your spiritual life will *always* be affected? Remember what we said about those key words or phrases that suggest extreme dichotomy. Stay away from them!

Part of Sandy's set-in-stone beliefs about being a failure at work occurred around a project that was not completed on time. She was the manager of the project. She was irresponsible. If she was irresponsible at work, that meant she must be irresponsible at home, with her friends, family, and in her relationship with God. She generalized this belief into every area of her life and believed she would always tend to be irresponsible. Sandy also had the tape of her father's shaming voice playing in her head. Nothing was ever good enough, and she just let her boss pick up where her dad left off.

If Sandy had demonstrated a "not everything" style, she might have been able to objectively conclude, "I am just not good at deadlines, but I'm great at managing my team, so I'll have to be more aware of time constraints." With this style, Sandy would be focusing solely on the work environment and not generalizing her irresponsibility to her home or relationships. The betrayed wife with an "explanatory"' style would believe that because her husband was unfaithful, it will affect everything in her life: her social world, her work life, and her spiritual life. Be wary of generalizing. Ask yourself if you have more of an "everything" or a "not-everything" style.

Unpacking Your Style

There is no right or wrong explanatory style. They are just different, and each holds different advantages and disadvantages. What's important is to develop a set of skills to allow our thinking to move from rigid to flexible. It's important to understand and pay attention to how your particular explanatory style and your set-in-stone beliefs are affecting your entire thinking process.

Over the past few decades, psychologists have recognized that when people experience situations that are out of their control, they tend to experience a feeling of helplessness. In 1965, Martin Seligman and his colleagues were doing research on classical conditioning, and they discovered why this was so. You may remember the concept from Pavlov's dogs if you took a Psychology 101 class. The idea was that animals (and humans) get "conditioned" to a stimulus (ringing a bell) and receiving a reward (getting food). The association of those paired stimuli cause the animal to make a response (salivate). After the pairing has occurred numerous times, the dog will salivate simply by hearing the bell ring.

Seligman's experiment was a little different. He included ringing the bell (stimulus) and giving the dog a mild shock. After a number of pairings, the animal reacted to the shock even *before* it actually occurred. In other words, as soon as the dog heard the bell, he acted as if he'd already been shocked. But Seligman took this a step farther. He put the animal in a large crate that was divided into two sections. On one side the dog could easily see a low fence that it could jump over if necessary. The floor on the one side of the fence had an electric current running underneath it.

Seligman put the dog on the electrified side of the fence and gave the dog a mild shock. He expected the dog would run over and jump the fence to the other side. To his surprise, the animal just lay down. He had been conditioned from the initial experiment that there was nothing he could do to avoid the shock, so he gave up in the second experiment.[5] This is called learned helplessness.

This makes a lot of sense for us as humans. If you think about all we've learned about the brain and attachment theory, you can easily see that the messages the brain has encoded about how life

THINK THIS **NOT THAT**

and relationships have worked out for us play a huge role in shaping whether or not we feel this learned helplessness.

Here's an example: imagine for a moment that you failed *again* in a current relationship. You could tell yourself several things about the relationship ending: "I'm a failure at relationships because I'm a lousy communicator." "I didn't try hard enough." "I'm a loser; that's why the relationship ended." With each of these statements you're making a different type of negative attribution. An attribution is simply the factor(s) that we use to place blame for the outcome of a situation. They can be made for positive and negative situations.

There are specific types of attributions that cause learned helplessness. Psychologists have categorized them into three areas: internal, stable, and global.[6] Using our above-mentioned example, telling myself that I failed in this current relationship because I'm a lousy communicator or I'm a loser is an internal attribution. I believe this is how I'm intrinsically wired (loser). If I had believed that the person I was in the relationship with was a loser, that would be an external attribution; then I'm blaming the other guy, which is out of my control.

If the attribution doesn't change over time, or it's fixed across circumstances, that makes it stable. For example, believing that I fail at relationships because I'm a bad communicator is a stable attribution, and it won't change just because of who I'm in a relationship with. Juxtapose that to believing that the reason you fail at relationships is because you don't try hard enough, or you don't want to learn how to communicate better.

If the attribution is global, this means that it affects many, or all, of the relationships I'm in, or could be in, not just one. Believing I can't communicate well says that this character flaw will be true about me in this current relationship and in all other future relationships I could potentially engage in. However, if I believe it was only specific to this relationship, then that would suggest that I may be successful at other relationships, just not this one.

Evaluate Worst Case Beliefs

To begin the evaluation process, we first need to record our set-in-stone beliefs about a given situation. If we continue with Sandy's set-in-stone beliefs about never getting a promotion no matter where she worked, most of us can agree that she is jumping to conclusions and generalizing. That is, we could safely conclude that just because she had a disagreement with her boss would not lead to her *never* being promoted in this job, or in any other job she had in the future.

Furthermore, if Sandy continues this line of negative thinking, she could easily begin catastrophizing. Here is an example of where she went with her negative attributions:

- I'm going to be fired.
- I will never get a good reference.
- I won't get another job.
- My kids won't be able to go to college.
- We'll end up living on the streets without two incomes.

If we could do a scan of Sandy's brain, it would show an abundance of limbic firing with increased blood flow to her amygdala. She would have a diminished flow to the prefrontal cortex areas as they begin to shut down logic and sound reasoning. Once our prefrontal cortex goes offline, the firing patterns throughout our subcortical areas then dominate our internal experiences, and we flip out.

So how do we actually shift our focus, bring our prefrontal cortex back on board, and achieve a more mindful state? Through reflection and what Dr. Siegel calls "mindsight" (as we'll see later). Here are his nine areas of prefrontal function.[7] We're going to use

Sandy's meltdown to map out her prefrontal cortex functions and see what happens in each area when we loose our minds.

1. Body Regulation

The mid-prefrontal region of the brain is responsible for the activity of a part of the nervous system that controls bodily functions, things like heart rate, respiration, and digestion. This "autonomic" nervous system is comprised of the sympathetic system (think of this as a car's accelerator) and the parasympathetic system (a car's brakes). Working in rhythm, they create balance in our bodies and help us to go from arousal to calmness. Left unchecked, we lose our minds. During Sandy's meltdown, her heart was racing at her anticipatory thoughts, her blood pressure would have been elevated, her breathing rapid, and her stomach was in knots—just as if she had been facing a true crisis.

2. Attuned Communication

Attunement to others shifts our internal state to resonate with the internal state of another. It's the foundation for empathy. When we freak out, get angry, panic, or whatever else revs up our limbic brain, we can no longer attune to others. We can't align with what they may be thinking or feeling. Sandy was so overwrought that instead of communicating with her boss and her coworker, she fled the scene.

3. Emotional Balance

This is a state of homeostasis. We aren't in emotional turmoil; we aren't spinning out of control; we are simply present, active, and alive. If we lack balance, we move in one of two directions: *chaos* or *rigidity*. Neither is good, and both can be draining in their own ways. We all get knocked off balance once in a while, but our prefrontal cortex has the ability to bring us back to a state of equilibrium. Remember, Stella couldn't get her groove back, and Sandy couldn't regain her equanimity after she began the journey down the road of imagined catastrophe.

4. Response Flexibility

This involves energy from the mid-prefrontal region. Siegel calls this the ability to pause before responding.[8] It's an important part of emotional and social intelligence. It helps us to be fully present to what is going on and to restrain ourselves from flipping out. It helps us consider other options. This often occurs when we are wronged in some way, and we replay the event in our minds over and over, and we feel ourselves start to boil all over again. This can cause us to lose control and say things we wouldn't ordinarily say or do. Fear works the same way. Sandy was motivated by the fear that she would lose her job and be out on the streets. The rising anxiety this caused made her act irrationally.

5. Fear Modulation

Fear is a powerful force, and while the fear center sits in the limbic brain, the mid-prefrontal cortex has direct connections to that area and is capable of modulating the firing of neurons in the amygdala. Empirical data has shown that we can consciously harness this connection to overcome fear by using our cortex to calm our limbic brain. This is done by a neurotransmitter called GABA (gamma-aminobutyric acid). Unlike other neurotransmitters, GABA plays an important role in the prefrontal inhibition of subcortical firing. If you have too much GABA, you can't get going. Too little, and your neurons are firing all over the map. If you've ever taken a Valium, you've experienced firsthand how it works with the GABA receptors to quiet your central nervous system. If you drink a lot of coffee, you can see the opposite effect. Coffee inhibits GABA, making you feel buzzed.

6. Empathy

This is the ability to be able to create a mental image of another person's mind. It's being able to label another person's internal world, to see things from their perspective. When our limbic area is on fire, we aren't thinking of anyone else but ourselves and our own needs.

7. Insight

By this we mean the ability to perceive our own internal world, to be aware of our own mind. We connect to the past and present, and we anticipate the future based on these mind maps. Again, the middle prefrontal cortex plays an important role in this process. When Sandy was having her meltdown, she was unable to put herself in the place of her coworker or her boss and slow down enough to consider how they might be feeling about the project being late.

8. Moral Awareness

This requires that we think in terms of the "bigger picture." Research has shown that this region becomes highly activated when we imagine actions for the larger social good. Other research has shown that when the middle prefrontal region is damaged, we become amoral.[9] When Sandy's PFC went temporarily offline, she was unable to see the bigger picture that went far beyond a couple of people's actions. She couldn't see how the company and her team would be affected by the project's not being completed. She was reactive and driven by her own feelings and fears.

9. Intuition

Siegel says this is how the middle prefrontal cortex gives us access to the wisdom of the body. He states:

> This region receives information from throughout the interior of the body, including the viscera—such as our heart and our intestines and gives us this input to give us a "heartfelt sense" of what to do or a "gut feeling" about the right choice. . . . Such intuition helps us make wise decisions, not just rational ones.[10]

Sandy had no access to her wise mind when this area of her brain was going haywire. When we are dealing with strong emotions, sometimes it's easy to rationalize our actions and decisions in the heat of the moment. The key is to hit the pause button, step back, and put on the brakes using the breath. Then we can make repair attempts and reconnect to ourselves and those we care about.

For Sandy, the incident with her boss and her coworker was only the tip of the iceberg. As I discussed these nine prefrontal functions with her, I zeroed in on point number five, fear modulation. On the surface, it seemed as if all Sandy was really concerned about was her boss and her coworker's unfair treatment of her. She was also deeply concerned about how they viewed her.

If we dig deeper into her story, however, we will see that there was a lot more going on than she realized. Sandy was dealing with unfinished business from her past. Her attachment wounds were constantly being reopened over and over by others in her world; she just had not ever made the connection. In those moments when her prefrontal cortex went offline, her limbic brain took over and her reactions were often over the top.

What Sandy didn't see was that she was reacting to the feelings, visual images, sensations, and words of her father who had shamed her on many occasions. When she was young, fear got attached to those original hurts and were the origin of much of her pain. It colored her life narrative and became the set-in-stone beliefs that she couldn't get out from under. "If my dad couldn't love me, no one else ever will. Therefore, others will abandon me because of my flaws," she said.

To protect herself, Sandy moved away from others to avoid the potential abandonment she so greatly feared. Because shame often makes its way into our narratives when we're young, and because children are egocentric in nature, it's easy to understand why children blame themselves and believe they are not "good enough" at such an early age. They don't have the ability to think abstractly or to think rationally.

Sometimes people even have no conscious recollection of these early shaming events. They simply respond by what is sensed in the body. Shame is a feeling that is intrinsic—it's associated with a person's sense of who they are. For Sandy, this translated into a felt sense of believing she was bad for most of her life. It's easy to see how toxic thinking and a false belief system can develop when people have been shamed. It's one of the most important topics we can expose and address today.

NOTES

[1]Reivich and Shatté, *The Resilience Factor*, 150.

[2]Reivich and Shatté, *The Resilience Factor*, 151–155.

[3]Reivich and Shatté, *The Resilience Factor*, 154–155.

[4]Reivich and Shatté, *The Resilience Factor*, 155.

[5]Natalie Boyd, "How Seligman's Learned Helplessness Theory Applies to Human Depression and Stress," http://study.com/academy/lesson/how-seligmans-learned-helplessness-theory-applies-to-human-depression-and-stress.html.

[6]Boyd, "How Seligman's Learned Helplessness Theory."

[7]Siegel, *Mindsight*, xii.

[8]Siegel, *Mindsight*, 27.

[9]Siegel, *Mindsight*, 29.

[10]Siegel, *Mindsight*, 29.

Chapter Seven

YOUR BRAIN ON SHAME

"Looking unto Jesus the author and finisher of our faith;
who for the joy that was set before him endured the cross,
despising the shame, and is set down at the right hand
of the throne of God."

—Hebrews 12:2 KJV

Dr. Brené Brown is a research professor at the University of Houston Graduate College of Social Work. She has spent the past decade studying vulnerability, courage, worthiness, and shame. Her 2011 book, *Daring Greatly,* was number one on the *New York Times* best seller list for over forty-eight weeks. How well her work has been received says something about how universal the problem is with shame and how hard we fight to keep it a secret. Not until we are willing to come out of hiding and talk about shame will we find freedom from the toxic thoughts and belief systems they engender.

I recently went to see the movie *Spotlight* with Mark Ruffalo and Rachel McAdams. It's the true story of how a team of investigative journalists from the *Boston Globe* uncovered a massive scandal of child molestation and cover-up within the local Catholic Archdiocese, shaking the entire Catholic Church to its core. It was a powerful and moving film. I came away from it with one word running through my mind—*shame.*

The Problem with Shame

What is shame? How does it affect us at the heart level? What does it do to our minds? What are the consequences of living with shame? What behaviors result from our carrying it? Can we ever be free from its grip? All important questions, and all questions that as a therapist I have wrestled with as I've walked alongside clients through these many years. I've also wrestled with them in my personal life as the wife of someone who committed suicide.

To help my clients, and myself, a journey of self-discovery is necessary. Growth comes as we decide whether the most important thing in our lives will be what happened to us, or what we chose to allow to happen in us as a result of the soul wound(s) we've incurred, because—let's face it—shame causes us to despise ourselves. I believe that at the heart of this monster we call shame there can be freedom, because Jesus himself scorned shame. The Bible urges us to fix our eyes on Christ, "the pioneer and perfecter of faith. For the joy set before him he endured the cross, *scorning its shame,* and sat down at the right hand of the throne of God" (Heb. 12:2, italics mine).

I don't know about you, but I always wondered what this passage really meant: Jesus *scorned the shame* of the cross. I suppose that it means that Christ himself, in human form, had feelings about shame. It's interesting that when tempted with the thoughts of feeling shamed, we read that Jesus *despised* it. Of all the words that could have been used to describe his feelings about overcoming shame, why did he choose that word? John Piper says this:

Shame was stripping away every earthly support that Jesus had: his friends gave way in shaming abandonment; his reputation gave way in shaming mockery; his decency gave way in shaming nakedness; his comfort gave way in shaming torture. His glorious dignity gave way to the utterly undignified, degrading reflexes of grunting and groaning and screeching. And he despised it. What does this mean?

It means Jesus spoke to shame like this: "Listen to me, Shame, do you see that joy in front of me? Compared to that, you are less than nothing. You are not worth comparing to that! I despise you. You think you have power. Compared to the joy before me, you have none. Joy. Joy. Joy. That is my power! Not you, Shame. You are worthless. You are powerless. You think you can distract me. I won't even look at you. I have a joy set before me. Why would I look at you? You are ugly and despicable. And you are almost finished. You cover me now as with a shroud. Before you can say, 'So there!' I will throw you off like a filthy rag. I will put on my royal robe."[1]

Here is Matthew Henry's take on this scripture:

He *endured the cross*—all those sufferings that he met with in the world; for he took up his cross betimes, and was at length nailed to it, and endured a painful, ignominious, and accursed death, in which he was numbered with the transgressors, the vilest malefactors; yet all this he endured with invincible patience and resolution. He *despised the shame* [italics mine]. All the reproaches that were cast upon him, both in his life and at his death, he despised; he was infinitely above them; he knew his own innocency and excellency, and despised the ignorance and malice of his despisers.

Why could Jesus scorn shame of the cross? Henry continues:

> What it was that supported the human soul of Christ under these unparalleled sufferings; and that was *the joy that was set before him.* He had something in view under all his sufferings, which was pleasant to him; he rejoiced to see that by his sufferings he should make satisfaction to the injured justice of God and give security to his honor and government, that he should make peace between God and man, that he should seal the covenant of grace and be the Mediator of it, that he should open a way of salvation to the chief of sinners, and that he should effectually save all those whom the Father had given him, and himself be the first-born among many brethren. This was the joy that was set before him.[2]

Jesus could scorn the cross and its shame because he held a bigger-picture mentality. He knew his suffering meant the redemption of mankind. He knew he was the fulfillment of the covenant of grace. He knew he would be the propitiation between God and mankind, and in this he could find inexplicable joy. He would give shame no foothold. He would give it no power, because he knew who he was and whose he was. So too should we despise this shame that seeks to dismantle us on every front because we also possess this inexplicable joy as the children of God.

The Narrative of Shame

"I feel so alone." "I hate my body." "I'm invisible." "I'll never be good enough." "I don't deserve . . . ." These are the voices of shame. The body collapses. The head hangs low. We feel constriction. There is heaviness in our soul. We feel hopeless. Shame waits there to devour us if we aren't careful. It's like someone took a sledgehammer to our soul. It leaves us with no choice but to turn inward.

Shame desires one thing: to enter our story and plant the lie. Fear sets in. Then comes the silence. Shame begets silence. Then we hide. Once shame has us isolated, it overtakes the soul. Destruction is inevitable. Death is often the result; if not a physical death, certainly a spiritual one.

So what is shame exactly? Is it simply a *feeling*? Or is there more to it? And what effects, if any, does shame's power exert over our brain? Shame by its very nature is hard to define. That's what makes it so insidious. I've seen it steal people's identity. I've seen it bring lives to absolute ruin. I've also seen it take life. It will stop at nothing to kill, steal, and destroy. That's its very intention, to rob God's creation of what is rightfully ours—a chance to understand and appropriate the identity of Christ and to walk securely in that truth.

Understand that shame is an *embodied* emotion, meaning that it is experienced holistically, in our body, soul, and spirit. Words like *humiliation, embarrassment,* or *disgrace* might help us connect to the felt experience of shame, but what does the mind do with it? What does the body do with it? How do I know the felt experience of shame is even what I'm feeling?

When an event occurs where one feels shame, the mind evaluates the external situation (what is causing the shame) and decides (prefrontal cortex) how to react (limbic brain), releasing the hormones and neurotransmitters that trigger the emotional response. The response itself, however, is expressed and felt in the *body*. It could look like anxiety, a depressed state, an avoidant state, a state of total emotional withdrawal. It can range from acute to chronic. Shame is always constricting. To counteract it, we have to create expansion in the system.

One of the main lessons of neuroscience that we've learned is that the power to focus and direct our attention shapes our brain's firing patterns. This felt experience of shame means neural firing is taking place in our brain, and neurons that fire together wire together. Thus, the pattern of shame embodies our being, and it's being installed in our neurocircuitry.

This is how it looked for a former client of mine whom we will call Jennifer. Jennifer came to see me because she was having anxiety and depressive issues. She had withdrawn from her family, her husband, her church, and her friends. When she came to see me, she revealed during our first visit that she was sexually abused as a child and carried a heavy burden of shame that she believed she had successfully buried.

As we know, when you bury things, you simply bury them alive, only to have them resurface at a later time. That's what happened to Jen. Her shame led her to a life of promiscuity that resulted in an unwanted pregnancy. At twenty-three, she had an abortion. She buried that too.

Jen found Jesus when she was thirty, got married a couple years later to a great guy, and had their first child three years later. That's when the bottom dropped out. She began having anxiety attacks and became very depressed. While I was taking her history, I asked Jennifer if she had ever had a significant traumatic event in her life. She denied that she had, but she told me that every September she would have these horrible episodes where she would usually end up in the hospital for a severe bout of depression and panic. One such episode had just occurred before she became my client.

I inquired again if there was anything in her past (besides the sexual abuse) that was traumatic. Perhaps something she had ignored, minimized, or was ashamed to tell me. Jennifer confessed that she had an abortion. I asked her when, and she said it was in September during her last year in college. So what was happening here? Jennifer was silently reliving the shame she had buried for so many years with the secret that she had kept hidden. Her physical body was reacting with anxiety and depression. Her symptoms were actually telling me something very deep and significant about shame; it was embodied, both in her mind and in her physical body.

Whatever words we use to connect with in regard to the felt experience of shame, one thing is certain: all shame begins with a *story*.

Every Picture Tells a Story

It took Jennifer twenty years to get to my office. There were times she wanted to see a therapist, but she always put it off for one reason or another, convincing herself that she just needed to "buck up" and get her stuff together. Through the many years, she realized she was depressed, but she had no idea how her depression was connected to her larger narrative.

During our initial visit, I asked her about her family of origin. She was reluctant to discuss her family, saying they had good and bad moments like everyone else does. What Jennifer was missing was the story shame was trying to tell as it weaved its way through her narrative.

Most therapists will tell you that ninety percent of our communication with others is conveyed nonverbally. Therefore, we must be mindful that the nonverbal communication we receive from the significant people who shape our world tells us a whole lot about who we are. If we feel shamed by a parent, for example, we may not express our feelings verbally, but the felt experience of being shamed is experienced through sensations, emotions, and thoughts.

It can look subtle—a disgusted glance from a parent, spouse, or friend—a harsh or sarcastic tone of voice, a dismissal, or a painful remark. It can also be profound like sexual abuse, infidelity, or emotional abuse. They all tell us the same thing: You are bad. You are unlovable. Something is wrong with you. Our responses to the shaming events in our lives, and what we do with them, have far-reaching consequences for us and for those with whom we engage in close relationships.

This was certainly the case for Jennifer. The more I listened to her story, the more convinced I was that it would take more than twenty milligrams of Paxil to fix what the years depression and anxiety had stolen from her. Shame had hijacked her prefrontal cortex, where reasoning, analyzing, and thinking gave way to the pull of her limbic brain (fight or flight). A steady diet of toxic thinking had Jennifer's body constantly revved up and focused on survival, thus she didn't have a prayer of growing healthy thoughts.

Jennifer grew up with a mother who was passive aggressive. She could be sweet but could turn around and make Jennifer feel punished if she didn't perform in the desired fashion. When Mom was displeased with Jen when she was little, Mom would get a disgusted look, roll her eyes, or a take on sarcastic tone.

As attachment theory tells us, the brain records these sensations, feelings, images, and thoughts, constructs meaning, and draws conclusions about the self. In Jen's mind, her shame followed the belief she repeated over and over in her mind—she was bad. It never occurred to her that there was a link between her mother's passive aggressive ways and how she thought about herself. While her mom never said Jennifer was bad, she got the message loud and clear that she was.

What Lies Beneath

We all experience feelings of shame at some time in our lives, and certainly not all the difficult moments we experience are rooted in shame. But it's safe to say that the "something is wrong with me" moments tell us in subtle whispers that we don't have what it takes to handle life, and that we are inherently flawed and inadequate. For Jennifer, the lie playing in her head said, "I am a person who is capable of doing something really bad, thus, it's true that I am bad, and something is inherently wrong with me." Having the abortion only solidified her already established belief that she was no-good.

For me, the shaming voice said, "You are responsible for Mike's death. If you had been a better wife, if you hadn't let him fly back from Florida alone that day, he wouldn't have died." The cognitive restructuring of those toxic thoughts was not enough to change my client's opinion of herself, or for me to change my beliefs about myself. Both Jennifer and I still *felt* that we were bad. While Jennifer came in presenting with panic attacks and depressive symptoms (which she did have), her primary problem was one of deep-rooted shame that couldn't be reduced by a few positive counterstatements or by that dose of antidepressant.

What both Jennifer and I needed was an *experience* with God. One where he would enter into the darkness with us and quiet the voice of judgment and condemnation we were placing on ourselves. The voice of the Judger is the voice of shame that appears on the home screen of our minds automatically and subtly. The associations connected to the Judger can be a parent, teacher, friends, or spouse. Interestingly enough, the loudest voice coming from the Judger is usually our own.

I talked to Jennifer about her concept of God. We used the practice of the spiritual disciplines to connect her to God. Once she was able to accept God's forgiveness and forgive herself for a choice that was inconsistent with her core value system, she was set free. She was able to change her attitude and be intentional about applying God's word to her life. Chemically, her brain (hypothalamus) would secrete the right amount of good chemicals (neurotransmitters) that would transmit electrical impulses for building healthy new thoughts.

If we look back at Sandy's experience with her boss from the previous chapter, we can see that some of these interactions that cause us to feel shame are the result of what *doesn't* happen in our life story. Sandy wanted something from her boss that she *didn't* get: praise. That loss was rooted in her original attachment wound from her father.

Not only did Sandy not get praise from her dad, she was repeatedly shamed. Whether it was impatience, a disgusted glance, or a harsh word, the message communicated was always the same: *Sandy didn't measure up.* That was the deeper piece that lay buried in her subconscious mind. She wanted something from her dad that she never got, and so that unfinished business from the past was still affecting her in the present as she tried to work that out through her boss.

Sandy didn't realize that what she was doing with her boss was the result of unfinished business with her dad. But as we talked about it, the light went on. She had the felt-experience of not being good enough for her father and, given her explanatory style (and her boss's style of interacting), Sandy got the subtle message that she wasn't good enough for him either.

Breaking Free

Sandy and I did a lot of work around her father issues. She began to realize that her felt sense of shame had permeated every relationship in her life, isolating her and causing her to speak, live, and act from a toxic lie-based system. Dr. Leaf weighs in from *Switch on Your Brain:*

> It's through the senses that we receive Satan's lies, but—
> and this is important—we don't have to believe those

lies. If we do believe them, we process them into physical realities . . . that form the substance of the nerve networks upon which we act. This means that if we listen to and believe the Enemy's lies, we actually choose to process them into physical realities inside our brains.[3]

That's the goal of the lie-based toxic thoughts of shame, to isolate and destroy, be it the individual mind or significant relationships.

I mentioned that in order to get our minds back on track, we need to practice reflection. One of the reasons this is critically important is that when we are dealing with issues like shame, which is an embodied emotion, no amount of talk therapy or theological facts are going to change a person's neuro-networks. Just as with Jennifer and myself, more was needed for Sandy.

That more was also an experience with God. I could tell Sandy all day long how beloved she was by God, how all the things her dad said were untrue, how her boss really did think she was an adequate employee, but at the end of the day, if she continued to tell the same story to herself, she would never be free. Keep in mind the brutal truth of shame's power lies in our fear of disconnection. The antidote for Sandy, and for all of us, is to have the courage to press through that fear and connect with God. He wanted to tell a new story for Sandy, a story of redemption, and I wanted to lay a foundation so that she could connect with him and he could begin his work on her new story.

I read Sandy the Hebrews 12 passage at the beginning of this chapter, the one that instructs us to "fix our eyes on Jesus." I told her we need to do what Jesus did to shame. We need to scorn it. We need to expose it. We need to have a willingness to be vulnerable before God and man and reframe our shame in light of the truth of who God says we are: his beloved. His sons and daughters. Adequate. Secure. Safe. If current neuroscientific research is telling us that our thoughts have the power to change our brains, then setting our minds on God's truth and telling ourselves what he wants us to hear will produce positive changes in our lives.

Hiding Place

The key to entering into the presence of God has at its core the idea of reflection. Here are some definitions of "reflection" from the *Merriam-Webster Dictionary*:

- "Something that shows the effect, existence, or character of something else."
- "A thought, idea, or opinion formed, or a remark made as a result of meditation."
- "Consideration of some subject matter, idea, or purpose."[4]

The heart of reflection can be summed up in one word—vulnerability. This may feel risky, but it's the only way to expose what has been hidden. Shame's power grows through secrecy and hiding. Lest you think shame is only experienced by those who have experienced abuse or trauma, think again. Take a look at the list below and see if any of these things have caused you to experience shaming thoughts.

- Your flaws were revealed.
- You are lacking at home.
- You are lacking in the workplace.
- You aren't enough in bed.
- You are never enough for your mom or dad.
- You don't have things under control at all times.
- No matter what you do, it's never quite good enough.
- You weren't popular.
- You are overweight.
- You didn't fit in.

- You aren't thin enough.
- You never got chosen (for the team, the squad, the home-coming court).

Perhaps you can think of a secret that you have worked very hard to keep under wraps, believing that if someone ever found out, you would be exposed and thus rejected. Here's what we all need to know: God is a seeker-God. He sought out Adam and Eve in the garden. He pursued them because he was more interested in a relationship with them than in what they had done wrong. God moved toward them. He asked them questions in the hope that the man and woman would be vulnerable before him. But fear's grip was too strong. The anticipatory feelings of felt-shame were too powerful. Thus, Adam and Eve hid from God and were banished from the garden forever.

And so it is with each of us who are in the stranglehold of shame's grip. We think toxic thoughts. We run. We hide. We keep secrets. All because of the terror we feel of being utterly exposed, abandoned, alone, or rejected—by others and by God. But rest assured, the body keeps score. All the stress hormones, all the fears, the worries, and the distorted thinking trigger degenerative processes that affect us body, soul, and spirit. While vulnerability may seem scary, the alternative of sitting alone with a sick mind and body is a lot scarier.

Dr. Brown explains in her book *Daring Greatly* what she believes to be the only path out of shame's insidious grip and the toxic thoughts and beliefs that come with it:

> As I look back on what I've learned about shame, gender, and worthiness, the greatest lesson is this: if we're going to find our way out of shame and back to each other, vulnerability is the path and courage is the light. To set down those lists of *what we're supposed to be* is brave.

To love ourselves and support each other in the process of becoming real is perhaps the greatest single act of daring greatly.[5]

Combating Shame

Let's say you muster up the courage to actually take up Dr. Brown on this idea of being vulnerable. What does it look like? How do you begin, especially if you've never done it or you're scared to death to try? Brown suggests we practice shame resilience. We've talked a lot about what characterizes resilient people, but let's take a look at what Brown says it looks like from her research. Speaking of shame resilience, she says,

> I mean the ability to practice authenticity when we experience shame, to move through the experience without sacrificing our values, and to come out on the other side of the shame experience with more courage, compassion, and connection than we had going into it. Shame resilience is about moving from shame to empathy—the real antidote to shame.[6]

Empathy is being able to put yourself in someone else's shoes and feel their pain. It's why we connect with books and movies on such a deep level, because other people's pain connects us with our own stories of sorrow and suffering. The sharing of our stories with others and feeling the presence of one another assures us that we are not alone. In my own journey, I had a strong support network of people who loved me and showed tremendous empathy toward me. Experiencing the compassionate presence of others, I am convinced, is the single most important key to healing.

The other critically important thing that I believe helped me to move forward after my husband's suicide was when I was able to show *myself* empathy and compassion. This was extremely difficult for me, but in time I began to be curious about this part of myself. How could I see myself as a compassionate person and not be willing to show that compassion to myself? Slowly, I was able to grow up that part of myself and show mercy to myself, given the trauma I had experienced.

I began paying close attention to the things that would trigger me, and I noticed I would always default to the negative thoughts. What I was telling myself placed me right back in shame's grip. I also started paying attention to the confluence of strength and struggle in my own body. How did it feel when I showed self-compassion? How did it feel when I allowed the toxic thoughts to inhabit my brain and my body? Could I find a softer, less judgmental way to speak to myself, one that would move me forward toward healing?

I also realized that healing didn't have to mean being pain-free; it meant I could hold both distress and growth simultaneously and still be okay. I could do this because I was well-supported by people who loved me. By examining my accusatory beliefs and being willing to modify them, reducing my expectations of myself, utilizing my strengths, and telling my story to a safe person, I was able to make progress. I also used Mike as a Remembered Resource Person during my trauma work and during this exercise and found tremendous healing. Let's take a moment and go through it.

Remembered Resource Person Exercise

This is an exercise I now incorporate into my therapeutic work because it was so healing for me. The point of the exercise is to have the Remembered Resource Person (RRP) speak truth into the wounded parts of you that need compassion, the parts that hold the guilt and shame. It is important to give these parts a voice, and this is a great way to do it.

An RRP is someone that knows you well and loves you unconditionally. It could be a spouse, friend, child, parent, the Holy
Spirit, or in my case, a deceased loved one (I used Mike). You are
going to have a conversation with this RRP and tell them about
your pain and knowing this person as well as you do, you're going
to listen carefully to see what they would say to you about whatever you're carrying.

So let's take a minute and try this. Let's use the Holy Spirit as
our RRP. I want you to think about something difficult in your
life, either past or present. Close your eyes and access that and see
what comes up. How does it feel in your body? Maybe you feel a
knot in your stomach, a tightness in your chest, or a heaviness in
your heart as you think about it.

Now I'd like to invite you to think about an emotion connected to this event that may need compassion. See if you can find
that part of self-compassion in your body. Notice any physical sensations that come with that—it may be warmth, it may be peace.

Now I'd like you to invite the Holy Spirit to speak to that part.
What would the Holy Spirit want to say to this part of you that is
needing compassion? Can you be connected to that part of yourself? Can you be curious about how this part can manifest for you
on a moment-by-moment basis? Can you remember that part is
always with you? No matter what tapes are playing in your head,
the truth comes from one source alone: the Holy Spirit. Receive
this and focus on it!

When I did this exercise during my trauma work, I imagined
what Mike would want me to know about the suicide being my
fault. Remember, I was drowning in guilt.

As you will see in the next chapter, it was a long and difficult
process, but I kept pushing forward.

NOTES

[1]John Piper, "What Does It Mean for Jesus to Despise Shame?," *Desiring God*, March 29, 2013, http://www.desiringgod.org/articles/what-does-it-mean-for-jesus-to-despise-shame.

[2]Matthew Henry, *Commentary on the Whole Bible: Complete and Unabridged*, second edition (Peabody: Hendrickson Publishers, 1991), 2403.

[3]Leaf, *Switch on Your Brain*.

[4]*Merriam-Webster*, s.v. "reflection," accessed October 10, 2017, http://www.merriam-webster.com/dictionary/reflection.

[5]Brené Brown, *Daring Greatly: How the Courage to Be Vulnerable Transforms the Way We Live, Love, Parent, and Lead* (New York: Avery/Penguin Group, 2012), 110.

[6]Brown, 74.

Chapter Eight

THE TOXIC EFFECTS OF TRAUMA ON THE BRAIN

The self who was in the camp isn't me, isn't the person who is here, opposite you. No, it's too unbelievable. And everything that happened to that other "self," the one from Auschwitz, doesn't touch me now, me, doesn't concern me, so distinct deep memory and common memory . . . without this split, I wouldn't have been able to come back to life.

—Charlotte Delbo, survivor of Auschwitz

I'm not afraid to die; I've already done that.

—Hugh Glass in *The Revenant*

No one wants to remember a trauma. To do so is having to speak of the unspeakable. But now, after three years, it's time to speak. At the beginning of this book, I mentioned that my husband committed suicide. What I didn't reveal was that I found him shot to death in our bed. If we're going to talk about exposing ourselves, risk being willing to be vulnerable, stepping out and being real, then I need to take the lead and share my story.

Trauma can do horrible things to the mind and body. The story I'm going to share with you will, I pray, help you find the courage to make your way out of the darkness if you've experienced a traumatic event. I also hope that it will allow you to see how the power of God can work to heal the mind. Before I begin to share the details of my story, let me start by giving you an overview about what trauma does to the brain.

In post-traumatic stress disorder (PTSD), which I was diagnosed with after the suicide, my brain experienced a crushing mental event that changed the entire course and meaning of my life, not to mention that it structurally altered my brain due to that medical word *neuroplasticity*. In the case of a traumatic event, neuroplasticity can work against the person who experiences the trauma because, as the person relives the event over and over, the memories become encoded deeper and deeper into the mind (remember: neurons that fire together wire together), thus disrupting normal brain function.

When a person is the victim of trauma or witnesses a traumatic event, the mind may not be capable of taking in the enormity of it. Therefore, the event isn't processed correctly. Telling the story of the traumatic event requires that the victim put words to what words can't describe. Many trauma victims often take years to articulate what happened to them. Memory lies in reexperiencing the horror and helplessness of the event through one's physical body.

Daring to Be Vulnerable: My Story

When faced with that which is beyond comprehension, we are cut off from the language needed to sort out the event. We are constantly fighting the urge to flee or freeze. In my case, I fled screaming at the top of my lungs from the bedroom where I discovered my husband, only to go downstairs and collapse on the floor into the fetal position. I have no recollection of running down the stairs, or of much that happened afterward. Time goes offline in the brain when a traumatic event is experienced.

My flashbacks would mirror both flight and freeze responses. From what we've learned so far about the brain, you can see that when something would happen to trigger a memory, my right (limbic) brain would react as if I was reliving the trauma in the moment. My rational left (MPFC) brain went totally offline. Total hysteria would take over, and I would run to the stairs before someone could apprehend me, thinking I could somehow run up to the bedroom and stop Mike from shooting himself. The flipside was curling up in a ball each time a flashback occurred.

Needless to say, the hormones that are secreted during a PTSD moment take a lot longer to return to baseline than normal, leaving the individual emotionally and physically wasted. Dr. Bessel van der Kolk explains this in his book, *The Body Keeps Score: Brain, Mind, and Body in the Healing of Trauma:*

> Dissociation is the essence of trauma. The overwhelming experience is split off and fragmented, so that emotions, sounds, images, thoughts and physical sensations related to the trauma take on a life of their own. The sensory fragments of memory intrude into the present, where they are literally relived. As long as trauma is not resolved, the stress hormones that the body secretes to protect itself keep circulating, and the defensive movements and emotional responses keep getting replayed.[1]

How Could Something So Right Go So Wrong?

Mike was my high school sweetheart. We had been happily married for thirty-eight years but together for forty-two. We had the normal ups and downs, disappointments, and sorrows that most people experience. But if you asked anyone who knew us, we had what most people only dream of. I adored him. He was a successful dentist with a thriving practice; I stayed home and raised our children.

Mike was a type-A personality. He was superman to everyone who knew him—especially to me. But superman forgot to tend to his own heart, and the fragmented parts of his life—those disappointments and losses he didn't process correctly—got buried in his subconscious for far too long. Early in 2013, he started becoming paranoid. He had always been untrusting of others, cautious and protective, but this was starting to get weird.

In August 2013, we took a trip to Arizona with my son and his wife. It was evident that things were clearly getting out of control. Mike was worried about people sabotaging his office, he thought people were planted at the restaurants we went to so they could watch him, and he was convinced the government was out to get him and put him in jail. It was bad. On several occasions he even accused me of being part of the conspiracy against him. I begged him to get help and referred him to one of my colleagues for an evaluation. He was prescribed medicine for depression and anxiety, and I found out later he never took it. When we came home from our trip, things went haywire.

One night I came home from work and thought he was asleep. I was working in the sunroom, and I heard a gunshot in the field. I ran through the house, screaming his name. Then outside. No answer. Our son drove up on his motorcycle, and then Mike came walking down from the field to the driveway with the gun in his hand. I was hysterical.

A couple of weeks later, he kissed me goodbye in the morning and never showed up for work. His office was worried because he didn't come in. I called my son, and we drove to the airport where Mike kept his airplane. I was sure he would be there. I was so filled with terror that I literally couldn't feel my arms.

After a long ordeal, we finally got a man to come and open the hangar. My son walked in, and I began screaming to him from the car. He called to me that his dad was in there and was okay. He had locked himself in the hangar and was sitting inside his car. It was at least 110 degrees in there, and he had been there for hours. I ran inside, collapsing to the ground, holding Mike's legs, and crying hysterically. When I stood up and looked at him, it was as if no one was there. He was blank, just staring into space. No emotion, no words. He was like a dead man.

We got him into the car, and I immediately called his psychiatrist. They said to take him right to the hospital, which we did. By then, he was fine. Laughing and joking. He told me not to say anything about suicide because he was afraid for his practice. Like a fool, I initially complied. Later, we met with a social worker to whom I told the entire story. They prescribed some medication for him, and we left.

There were several more incidents when he attempted to shoot himself, times I was unaware of. He told me of one. Every time he was late or didn't show up somewhere, I was hysterical. The torment never stopped. One night he told me that it was really hard to kill yourself. He pulled a gun out and, as we sat in bed, he put it to his side and told me how he watched the bullet go into the chamber (on this particular gun you could actually see the bullet in there). I was crying and begging him to stop. I told him he was terrifying me.

None of us believed he actually would take his life. Not even his psychiatrist. One night while we were lying in bed, he told me that he never could really kill himself because he couldn't leave me, and he wouldn't ever want to leave me with such a mess. My mistake was to believe him.

A Final Plea

I called a dear pastor friend of ours for an intervention. I was so desperate. Larry spent three hours with Mike, and Mike never told him of his suicidal thoughts. He was drowning in shame. I walked into their conversation because we had an appointment at an outpatient treatment facility we were going to look at, and we needed to leave. I asked Larry if Mike had told him about his paranoia and the suicidal thoughts. He said no. Mike told Larry he didn't need or want to go for treatment, he was only doing it for me. I was furious!

I felt like he didn't want to help himself or me. His behavior was getting more and more aberrant, and I was scared. Mike was such a strong, self-sufficient man. He was the strongest man anyone knew. That was the problem: heroes seldom ask for help. Parts of him had been mortally wounded in life, and for the most part he did a good job of hiding them.

He actually did make the appointment at Dominion Hospital that day. I had been so frustrated and exhausted that I went upstairs before Larry left and fell asleep. Mike left without me. He called me from the hospital, and I told him that if he didn't get some help, I was done. He said he did want to get help, and he did go the following day for the in-patient program. He didn't last but half the day. He was very disappointed with the group they put him in. It was all teens, he told me. He was in such despair because he really thought it would help. I said I'd find something else for us to try.

Mike was getting progressively worse. We took a trip to Sedona with my son and his wife, and it was evident that Mike's ability to think rationally was slipping away. My son was deeply concerned. Mike was so paranoid. He and I went out to dinner one night, and he told me the waiter and the couple sitting next to us were planted there at the restaurant to watch him. There was no reasoning with him. He was sure that his office was being watched and that people were out to get him.

By now you're probably wondering why we didn't commit him, but Mike had always been overly careful, protective, a little paranoid, and untrusting of people. Many of the things he came up with were not beyond belief. The kids actually believed most of what he said in the beginning. But none of us believed he would ever take his life. Even his psychiatrist said Mike was a person who wanted to live. "He's impulsive, but he wants to live." I suppose you can imagine the guilt I struggled with. Mike and I had a unique love story. We were Romeo and Juliet. We never wanted to be without each other. My brain couldn't make sense of all this. That's the bad thing about traumatic events; they seldom provide closure for those left behind. To this day, it's no more real than when it was happening.

Running for My Life

We took a short trip to Florida with friends, and the weekend went south quickly. He was paranoid, depressed, and highly anxious. I sat with him and tried to comfort him and assure him that going to Meier Clinics in Dallas would help him. He needed medication and at this point was open to considering it.

He left Monday morning to fly back to DC, and I would come home Tuesday. The plan was that I would meet him in Dallas over the weekend and would stay with him while he attended the day program as long as was necessary. Monday night we spoke on the phone, and he sounded down. I asked him to call me when he got to Dallas and let me know he was safe. He said he would. Little did I know that would be the last time I would hear his voice.

I sat in the airport in Ft. Lauderdale, waiting to fly home. I was like a madman. I must have called a thousand times starting on Tuesday morning. Mike never picked up his cell. I was extremely anxious and called my son. No answer. Then I called our daughter. I was upset because I thought something I said to him on the phone might have upset him. I also felt terribly guilty that I didn't go back home with him and then fly to Dallas with him.

He wasn't sure he would get the help he needed there. He had already tried one place in Northern Virginia and only lasted half a day. I told him to go Tuesday and try it out for a few days, and if he thought it was a good fit, I'd fly there Friday, and we would stay as long as necessary. Finally, as I sat pacing in the airport, I remembered the name of the clinic he was going to so that he could get his blood work results and take them along to Dallas. The woman I spoke to said he had kept the appointment! I felt like a million tons had been taken off me.

He never made it to Dallas.

I landed at Reagan Airport just as if it was any other trip back from our Florida home. I stood outside waiting for a taxi. During the ride home, I tried calling him again. No answer. I spoke with my daughter-in-law and decided I would go over to their house to ease my nerves after I dropped off my bags at the house.

When the cab pulled up in the driveway, I noticed the garage door was up, and I saw Mike's car. I figured he must have called a cab to go to the airport. When I walked into the house, I saw his leather bag and his Bible on the counter. Now I started to panic. I ran through the kitchen and up the stairs calling his name. When I turned the corner from the stairs, I had full view into the bedroom and could see his form from way down the hall. I don't remember anything else but touching him and seeing all the blood. I knew he was dead, but it wouldn't compute in my mind. As I said, I left the room running for my life and screaming.

After the trauma, I experienced my world very differently. My nervous system was either on high alert, or I was a zombie. My energy became focused on suppressing the horrific memories. Flashbacks, which occurred daily, served to strengthen the neurocircuitry in my brain, making it more and more difficult to function.

Shame and guilt were annihilating my mind. I couldn't get out of bed. I remember almost nothing of those days, weeks, months. My thoughts were toxic. I blamed myself. It was my fault. I caused this to happen to him because I didn't do what I should have done (remember the shoulds, musts, and oughts from the cognitive distortion list). I didn't want to live. Anything and everything would trigger a flashback. Dr. van der Kolk weighs in:

> Since at least 1889, when the French psychologist Pierre Janet published the first scientific account of traumatic stress, it has been recognized that trauma survivors are prone to "continue the action, or rather the (futile) attempt at action, which began when the thing happened." Being able to move and *do* something to protect oneself is a critical factor in determining whether or not a horrible experience will leave long-lasting scars.[2]

Mapping a Meltdown

Below you will find seven of the nine prefrontal functions outlined by Dan Siegel in his book *Mindsight*.[3] We'll look at each of them to see how I reacted during my flashbacks. I will also list some of the skills I developed to cope with the traumatic memories.

1. Body Regulation

My sympathetic nervous system was on overdrive, as evidenced by shaking, hysteria, rapid heartbeat, nausea, derealization, and catatonia. It was very difficult to engage my parasympathetic system to calm myself.

Strategies I used for change:

Deep breathing (to engage the parasympathetic system).

Body Scan—to recognize tension before and shift to relaxation.

Focusing exercises.

Going to the safe place I had constructed in my mind to ground myself (more on that later).

Grounding techniques, which included slapping my hands together with force and rubbing them together to create heat in my palms. This helped to ground me to the here and now.

Using tangible objects (I had several that helped) to rub, hold, or caress for self-soothing and grounding.

Reading my Bible.

Writing in my journal.

2. Attuned Communication
I needed the attuned, compassionate presence of friends and family when I reentered the traumatic moments, but I couldn't align my emotional state with others because my prefrontal cortex went offline so often and prohibited me from receiving what I needed. It would take time before I could even realize others were present there beside me during a Post Traumatic episode.

Strategy I used for change:
Because my loved ones stuck with me through these episodes, over and over, and because I practiced my grounding and breathing skills, I was eventually able to reconnect to myself and subsequently to others. People would literally have to pick me up and make me walk around or go outside to take a twenty-minute walk.

3. Emotional Balance
I had none, especially in the first few months. I moved toward total chaos in my state of continual hyperarousal. Then I would become depressed. Remember, the amygdala communicates with the hypothalamus (the command center), which secretes chemicals based on what's going on in your thought-life. Worried thoughts get the hypothalamus producing more chemicals than are necessary. The amygdala is also connected to the PFC where

our reasoning and rational thinking take place. If we stop thinking a toxic thought, it dissipates. This enables us to balance our emotions and respond appropriately. If we don't stop thinking toxic thoughts, the information gets sent to the hippocampus which is responsible for encoding information and seeing if it will get a permanent place in our memory banks.

Strategies I used for change:
Once my MPFC brought me back to a state of equilibrium as I used my calming techniques, I could ask for what I needed from others. Calming myself allowed me to move from chaos to a more balanced state. Deciding not to think, or, should I say, deciding not to receive the toxic thoughts as truth was my biggest challenge. Other things I would do to achieve emotional balance were to connect to my safe place, practice focusing techniques, and write in my journal daily.

4. Response Flexibility

During that first year, I had no ability to pause before a trigger went off in my brain and set off an episode. That's what's so terrifying about trauma. Things I thought would be difficult sometimes weren't, and other things I didn't even think about turned out to trigger some of my worst episodes. Response flexibility enables us to be aware of what's happening and restrain our impulses.

Strategy I used for change:
As time has gone on, and with lots of trauma work behind me (EMDR), I now have the increased self-awareness to sense when emotions are rising or when I'm moving toward chaos. Those cues help me to pause and pay attention to what's going on in my internal world. Then I can use my skills. Don't get me wrong, sometimes I'm just a hot mess. Just because I'm a therapist doesn't mean I do this right every time. Allow yourself grace.

5. Fear Modulation

Beside the fact that I walked into such a horrific scene with the suicide, old fears that arose from this event began resurfacing. Fear of being alone. Fear of despair and anxiety returning. Fear of wanting to take my own life. Once my amygdala was hijacked, my limbic brain had no problem taking over and reexperiencing the terror of that afternoon. Fear pretty much ruled my life in every aspect.

Self-understanding. The associations that I made as a result of the trauma (loss of security) put my limbic brain on high alert. Time is also frozen during traumatic events, so when I have a thought, it's as if I'm experiencing it in the here and now. The fact that my husband was gone triggered other emotional issues in my life that I needed to reflect on and make sense of. Making sense of our stories gives us deeper understanding of ourselves and our connection to others. I also had to choose to reject the activated thoughts and information coming into my mind. This was incredibly hard work.

Strategy I used for change:
The only antidote to fear is faith. I devoured God's word. I couldn't pray, but others prayed for me constantly. I used the breathing and grounding techniques to calm myself, but it took a long time for the fears to dissipate. The presence of God and the presence of others who loved me helped to make me feel safe and calmed my fear.

6. Empathy

During my recovery, I couldn't even see anyone else's pain, regretfully, not even the pain borne by my kids. I couldn't attune to their pain. I was so consumed with the enormity of my grief and the horror of the event that simply surviving became a full-time job. I had absolutely nothing to give to anyone.

Strategy I used for change:
The only solution for a trauma victim is to keep putting one foot in front of the other. Right after the tragedy, I got into therapy, I joined a suicide-support class and a small group, and I also began attending a grief group at my church. There, with other suicide survivors and among those who had experienced loss, I was able to give and receive empathy by listening to the stories of others' integration. I listened to Scripture, I read my Bible, and eventually I began going out. I tried to restore as much normalcy to my life as I could, but this took a lot of time.

7. Insight

Insight is the ability to perceive and monitor our own internal world as well as that of others. We use our observations about our current life-state as well as the past to anticipate and even predict what we will experience in the future. After the trauma, I had a tremendous amount of fear of the future. As time progressed, it became harder and harder not to let that fear completely rule my thinking. I thought I might take my own life; I thought I would face financial hardship; I thought I would never recover. I could barely wrap my mind around my own thoughts because they were so distorted, much less put myself in anyone else's shoes. My internal world felt like total chaos.

Strategy I used for change:
The insight necessary to key into others' feelings took time. I know I must have hurt people's feelings and neglected people, but I seriously had trouble getting outside myself. I found myself being forgetful, feeling numb, and more and more disoriented. Time helped me gain insight, especially into my own internal world. Through my personal therapy work, I was able to release some of the guilt I carried by considering some of the concepts I've

presented here in this book. I still struggle, I still hurt, I still have days when I'm overwhelmed and don't want to go forward, but I press on because Jesus has promised me eternity, and I believe my work here is not complete. If I can choose to look through a different lens to navigate through what has happened to me, I want to be a voice that says, you can do it too. Never give up! The story isn't finished yet!

I would love to tell you that I'm totally healed, that I never have a toxic thought or flashback. That's not the case. With time and intentionality and the grace of God, I have learned to manage my PTSD moments pretty well. As I write this, next week it will be three years since that awful day. This has been a very difficult month for me. Some days are still unbearable. That is because the greater the attachment to that which we love, the greater the loss. Thank God for my faith and for the promises I have. Not only do they give me hope, but they help me to work hard at building a new memory base.

NOTES

[1]Bessel van der Kolk, *The Body Keeps Score: Brain, Mind, and Body in the Healing of Trauma* (New York: Viking/Penguin Group, 2014), 66.

[2]van der Kolk, 55.

[3]Siegel, *Mindsight*, xii.

PART THREE

REWIRING

Chapter Nine

BUILDING A NEW MEMORY BASE

Do not conform to the pattern of this world,
but be transformed by the renewing of your mind.

—Romans 12:2

Dr. Aaron Beck and Dr. Albert Ellis designed worksheets for clients to track their dysfunctional thinking. Remember, Ellis believed people caused themselves excessive amounts of stress by "awfulizing" the situations and events of life. The worksheet created by Beck, the Dysfunctional Thought Record (DTR), does a couple things.

First, as I mentioned before, using his DTR is a good brain exercise, because writing things down helps promote right- and left-hemisphere integration which, as we've seen, is very important.

Second, it helps increase your self-awareness by helping you track and identify thoughts, feelings, beliefs, and thinking errors. It helps you learn to pay attention to and label your internal world by writing down what you're feeling. It also lets you practice shifting your thinking by creating positive counterstatements to refute the old dysfunctional thought patterns. When practiced daily, this is another way the rewiring process takes place.

Crafting a Dysfunctional Thought Record

I have come up with my own version of the DTR, and I give it to all my clients because it's a great way to take all I've taught them and put it into practice. A copy of my DTR is included on the next page. It's a most necessary practice in building a new memory base and learning to rewire the brain. Let's take a look. I'm going to use my story after the suicide to help you see how toxic thinking began for me after Mike's death.

After the trauma I was in shock, but once that wore off, the guilt and shame set in with a fury, seeking to destroy my soul. I tasted despair to the point of wanting to end my own life. My set-in-stone beliefs were as follows:

- It's my fault.
- I should never have let Mike fly back home alone that day. If I had come home with him, he wouldn't have done this.
- I should have said something different to him the night before on the phone, and he'd still be alive.
- I killed my husband.
- I can't live without Mike.
- I'll never make it through this.

On the next page, I've diagramed this on the DTR so you can see how toxic thinking leads to toxic beliefs, which in turn leads to destruction.

It's important to note that while most of us think our situation causes our feelings, the truth is, our thoughts and beliefs drive everything. Remember, our feelings and our actions will always follow what we're believing in any given situation.

Dysfunctional Thought Record

Situation →	Thoughts →	Beliefs →	Feelings
Mike takes his life	It's my fault	I'm responsible	Shock
	I'm bad	I must die too	Guilt/Shame
	I won't get over it	I won't make it through this	Terror
	I did this to him		Despair

Now let's look back and see how the last few months Mike and I had together influenced me in the present, making the situation I found myself in more emotionally charged.

Original Hurts ←	Fear/Belief →	Coping →	Thinking Errors
Mike refuses help	I'm alone	Try harder	Negative thinking
	He doesn't care about me	Be angry	Personalization
	He won't fight for us	Control	Should statements
			Emotional Reasoning

Putting both the diagrams together is what comprises my unique version of the DTR. I want my clients to look at the whole picture, past and present, as they work at becoming more self-aware. I want them to identify false beliefs, thinking errors, their original hurts (attachment wounds), fears, and what coping strategies they have employed to manage their pain. I want them to zero in on how all of this is affecting them in the present moment with the situation(s) they are confronting. I also want them to come up with some positive counterstatements to replace their negative thoughts.

As you can see from my diagram, I had a lot of stuff going on in my head. The last three or four months with Mike were a living hell. His refusal to get help or to take the prescribed medication for his increasing paranoia and depression was very frustrating. He was severely depressed in the last few weeks, to the point where he could not function. I was on 911 alert all the time. He tried several times to take his life before it actually happened, but I believed deep in my heart (we all did) that he would *never* do it.

I believed him because, to me, he was superman. There wasn't anything he couldn't do or overcome. I'd seen it for more than forty years. During those last months, I was constantly being terrified by his actions, but things were so intense that I didn't have time to process my own feelings. I was always on high alert. I was angry at him because he wasn't being honest about what was going on inside him. He wasn't telling the truth. He wasn't taking his meds. He wasn't honest with the doctor or with others who were trying to help him.

It was an emotional rollercoaster. I was angry one minute and trying to save him the next. I begged him to get help. He finally agreed, but I don't know if he really believed he could be helped. I think he was too tired and just gave up. The mental illness took over. Remember, what happens for us, and what happened to me, is that fears become attached to the hurts we experience in our lives. Those fears, and the hurts that lie underneath them, become the catalyst for the belief systems we develop.

For me it looked like this:

- Fear/Belief: Mike doesn't care enough to fight for our relationship.
- I'm responsible for Mike getting better.
- I can't trust him to take responsibility for his own care.

Because I felt so responsible for him, when I messed up and didn't fly home with him, my set-in-stone belief that I was responsible for his suicide was as real for me as if I had pulled the trigger for him. It was *all* my fault. I was a terrible wife.

There is one more thing I include in my DTR, and that's to have clients list their cognitive distortions (thinking errors). For me it looked like this:

- Personalizing: Not only was I blaming myself for the suicide without considering his role; I was blaming myself for not being a good enough wife.
- Emotional Reasoning: Not only did I feel guilt and shame. I was now someone whose stupid mistake cost her husband his life. I was a horrible human being.
- I was drowning in the *should* statements. "I should have flown back with him." "I should have known he would take his life." "I should not have said some of the things I said. I should have been a better wife." All of this compounded my despair.
- Negative Self-Defeating Thinking: All the horrible thoughts that tormented me then, and sometimes creep back up even now, did *not* help me move forward. They were not helping me get where I needed to go. They were only burying me in a sea of despair. I had to decide how long I was going to allow this toxic thinking to cloud my vision.

The Crazy Cycle

Let me walk you through a few incidents that took place during that three-to-four-month crazy cycle with my husband to show you how his catastrophic thinking contributed to his mental demise. Mike was always a person who was cautious about life. His childhood messages taught him that the world wasn't a particularly safe place and others weren't trustworthy. Mike didn't find a safe base and secure haven in his parents. He had seven brothers and sisters, and there wasn't much to go around in the way of nurturing. He had some deep attachment wounds. More than I ever realized. He was a sensitive person who learned to put up a strong front. He played the "hero" role in his family and was great at fixing and rescuing everyone—except himself.

He grew up with a set-in-stone belief that you have to take care of yourself because others won't be there for you. When he met my parents at seventeen and they showed him such unconditional love, that was a game-changer for him. But he still wrestled with demons inside. He was betrayed by many, and he dealt with his pain by stuffing it. Since he was the hero, he couldn't be vulnerable. His job was to rescue and fix others. He and I had our rough patches, just as any couple. In fact, we had just come out of a difficult time in our marriage the previous year. The last year was amazing, but my career, the kids, his personal demons, and extenuating family issues all took their toll on his heart.

In the last year of his life, Mike became highly suspicious of the things that were going on around him. Looking back, I now see that I never realized how all of this was progressing into complete paranoia. He installed cameras all over our homes and property. He believed the FBI was watching him. His malpractice insurance got cancelled, his airplane insurance got cancelled, and Medicare was doing a routine check in his office because he was the only dentist in a two-hundred-mile radius that would tend to the poor. He attributed all this to a conspiracy. Several times he insinuated that I was in on a conspiracy against him.

By now you should be able to see how and why things got so out of hand in Mike's mind. Because he didn't really trust people, his mind took him right back to earlier attachment wounds. They had become raw spots in his heart. Siegel weighs in from *The Mindful Therapist*:

> If you have had repeated experiences of being unseen or mistreated or betrayed, you are more likely to be vigilant for these examples of misattunement, perhaps seeing them readily, or even imagining them when they in fact are not really occurring. Understanding your own history is crucial so that you are aware how trust and mistrust have played important roles in your life.[1]

Here's where mindfulness comes in. Again, Siegel comments:

> We are looking for historically created and presently enacted adaptive strategies in response to mistrust as an important inner exploration that can illuminate how vulnerability and trust are unfolding now. These are aspects of an inner narrative that can be explored in journal writing or walks in nature: What were the patterns that you adopted to deal with betrayals of your trust? How did you respond to being ignored, intruded upon, or terrified? In what ways did your development since childhood become influenced by times when others let you down? What role does vulnerability play in your life now?[2]

These are important questions to consider because they reveal why we think, act, and behave the way we do. The problem is that most of us are afraid to dig deep, reflect, and be vulnerable—even with ourselves. Our lack of self-awareness perpetuates the cycle of toxic thinking. Toxic thoughts place excessive stress on the brain. They actually cause the hippocampus to lose cells and change shape. When we don't pay attention to how our personal narratives have shaped our thought-life, we are doomed to stay stuck in the same patterns of negative thinking.

I will never know if Mike's toxic thinking led to the changes in his brain chemistry (I'm convinced it contributed), or if there was something else seriously wrong. There are lots of theories out there, especially given that he was a dentist and breathed in the fumes from the mercury for twenty-five years. I agonized and theorized about all of it.

Still today there is no closure. When someone commits suicide, all the psychological baggage they carried is placed on the survivor(s). I will carry that until the day I die. I can still feel the effects of the trauma on my brain. The surrealness of the tragedy, the dissociation, the inability to fully integrate it into my current life schema, the occasional flashbacks, and the toxic thinking that tries to pull me backwards. If I don't guard my thoughts—and I do have the ability to choose them—I will fall into that dark abyss of despair that held me powerfully in its grip.

Thankfully, God has given me a healing touch, and I cling to it with every fiber of my being. I know how much Mike loved and served the Lord. He was a great man. But he was still a man, not the superman that I and so many others made him out to be. Even superman needs to guard his heart. Even superman needs to examine and explore those parts of himself that are hidden. And even superman needs help sometimes.

By the time Mike asked for help, he was so far gone mentally that some are convinced he would never have made it back. I disagree. But it doesn't matter now. It's over. You and I have a *choice*. If we can sit back and observe our thoughts, we can harness the power of learning to redirect them away from the negative to the positive. Dr. Leaf calls our attention to how this looks neurobiologically:

> Proteins are made and used to grow new branches
> to hold your thoughts. So, if you don't get rid of the
> thought, you reinforce it. This is phenomenal because
> science confirms that you can choose with your free
> will to interfere with genetic expression, which is pro-
> tein synthesis. If you say you can't or won't, this decision
> will actually cause protein synthesis and change in your
> brain into "I can't" or "I won't."[3]

For Mike, all the demons he was fighting told him he couldn't overcome the thoughts and beliefs he held, and his superman personality told him he wouldn't get help—that he could do it himself. You can see how those thoughts and beliefs only reinforced the toxic neuropathways.

I saw how the power of God's Word would transform Mike's thinking each time I would read him Scripture, or when we would talk about who he was and what he believed. I watched the light come back on in his heart. But the Enemy was relentless, torment-ing his mind and thoughts so that he couldn't hold on to the truth. Truth must be reinforced to create change.

God thought that transforming and renewing our minds was so important he gave us several verses in Scripture to consider. If you are struggling with depression, anxiety, or hopelessness, remember the words of your heavenly Father. You may even want to commit to them to memory. (Note the phrases I have empha-sized in each passage.)

> Do not be conformed to this world, but be transformed
> by the *renewal of your mind*, that by testing *you may*

discern what is the will of God, what is good and acceptable and perfect. (Rom. 12:2 ESV)

Though we walk in the flesh, we are not waging war according to the flesh. For the weapons of our warfare are not of the flesh but have *divine power to destroy strongholds*. We destroy arguments and every lofty opinion raised against the knowledge of God, *and take every thought captive to obey Christ*, being ready to punish every disobedience, when your obedience is complete. (2 Cor. 10:3–6 ESV)

You keep him in perfect peace whose *mind is stayed on you*, because he trusts in you. (Isa. 26:3 ESV)

To set the mind on the flesh is death, but to set *the mind on the Spirit is life* and peace. (Rom. 8:6 ESV)

The *peace* of God, which surpasses all understanding, will *guard your hearts and your minds in Christ Jesus*. (Phil. 4:7 ESV)

But we have the mind of Christ. (1 Cor. 2:16 ESV)

Toxic-thinking patterns keep us imprisoned in the same old thought patterns and behavioral strategies. The question is, how well are they working? Answer: they aren't. Therefore, we have to make a decision if we want to change, and if we do, we have to recognize that it's going to be hard work.

Presence

As I began to do my therapeutic work, I realized these self-defeating patterns of thinking and relating were never going to help me grow and move forward. As I learned to monitor my internal world and be present with myself, I learned to be aware of the times that trust was not present in my life and how those old thought patterns affected me.

I didn't want to avoid what was painful. I was pressing into the idea of being comfortable being uncomfortable. I learned to differentiate between what I was consciously aware of—things like my anger, my feelings of betrayal, the hurt and grief. I also learned more about the experience of awareness itself.

To begin expanding on the idea of self-awareness, I had to do what I explained in the previous chapter—become more self-aware of my body and my thoughts. I had to learn to monitor my internal world and be wary of fortune telling. When people experience a lot of negative circumstances in their lives, it's easy to begin believing that a dark cloud is always following them around. You are always waiting for the next calamity. How do we harness the power of becoming self-aware? One word. Focus. Let's take a look.

NOTES

[1]Daniel Siegel, *The Mindful Therapist* (New York: W. W. Norton, 2010), 76.
[2]Siegel, *The Mindful Therapist*, 79.
[3]Leaf, *Switch on Your Brain*.

Chapter Ten

HARNESSING THE POWER OF FOCUSED ATTENTION

Let this mind be in you, which was also in Christ Jesus.

—Philippians 2:5 KJV

We have the mind of Christ.

—1 Corinthians 2:16

Finally, brothers and sisters, whatever is true, whatever is noble, whatever is right, whatever is pure, whatever is lovely, whatever is admirable—if anything is excellent or praiseworthy—think about such things.

—Philippians 4:8

What do you think Paul meant when he said, "We have the mind of Christ"? As you think about this, notice that he doesn't say, you can *get* the mind of Christ, you have to *struggle* to have the mind of Christ, or you have to *imitate* the mind of Christ. He is saying that we *have* the mind of Christ, if the Spirit of the living God dwells within us. All that Christ is—his nature, his character, his very mind, and his very life—is available to the one who chooses to appropriate it. If we chose to appropriate this truth and focus on it, the result will be inner peace.

Consider this: if I had an expensive watch, and you loved watches, and I wanted to give it to you as a gift, what would you do? Would you resist my generous offer? You might for a minute or two, but eventually you would reach out (action), take, and receive the gift. That is what Paul is saying in the above-mentioned verse: let the mind of Christ live in and through you moment by moment, and let this rule your life. Accept this gift. Use this gift. In order to make the most of it, you have to focus on it daily, especially when you are beset by all manner of evil, when you are hard-pressed on every side, when you are weary and want to quit—accept what God has given.

To "have the mind of Christ" means to arm yourself with the attitude of Jesus described in Philippians 2:5–8:

> In your relationships with one another, *have the same mindset as Christ Jesus:* Who, being in very nature God, did not consider equality with God something to be used to his own advantage; rather, he made himself nothing by taking the very nature of a servant, being made in human likeness. And being found in appearance as a man, he humbled himself by becoming obedient to death—even death on a cross! (italics mine)

This is why you have Christ *in* you, fellow-struggler. It's his power, his strength, the indwelling of the Holy Spirit, his life, that allow us to change. Do you believe that? You will only experience the mind of Christ to the degree that, first, you believe in the total goodness of God's nature and character, and second, if you accept it as true and appropriate it for your own life. If you don't believe it, then you won't be able to harness what is available to you.

In order to rewire your brain, you have to focus. I think I've made that pretty clear throughout this book. To focus, you need practice. We've already looked in Chapter Three at a jillion ways your mind can be distracted in today's noisy world. In this chapter, I want to teach you how focused attention can actually promote integrative changes in your brain.

If we're honest, most of us have a hard time staying focused for long. We cringe at the thought of sitting still for too long because we might have to come face-to-face with ourselves. Learning to fix our attention can harness all kinds of awareness in our lives. It also will help us to calm troubling emotional states instead of being overwhelmed by them. This is a powerful concept, especially for those of us who have been traumatized or for those who struggle with other mental health issues, like my friend Patrick.

When Your Mind Feels Like a Wrecking Ball

Patrick was seventeen when he came to see me because he was depressed. He was a tall, lanky, and handsome kid, but, of course, he didn't think so. He struggled with low self-esteem, shyness, and bouts of social anxiety. His parents were concerned because he was becoming more withdrawn, and his grades were taking a nosedive. I asked him the usual questions about his home-life, and he reported it had been "fine." I didn't believe a word of it, but I wasn't about to press him for details just yet.

Patrick did tell me he had been feeling pretty down. His parents were divorced, and he was living between both homes. He said it sucked. What I did find out was that he was having bursts of anger juxtaposed to what he called "crying jags." Sometimes he would have bursts of energy and feel like he could conquer the world. He'd stay up all night with his friends, and sometimes he'd do wild and crazy things. Then a week later, it seemed as though he would crash and burn. During those times, he'd have the crying spells. He told me he had thoughts of taking his life. He had even tried self-harming on several occasions.

Patrick was a really cool kid. I liked him instantly, but I was concerned for him, as was his family. I wasn't sure if Patrick was bipolar, or just anxious and depressed, but either way I knew some focusing techniques would be beneficial for him. He told me his mind felt like a "wrecking ball." When I asked him to explain, he said he felt these crazy swings in his mood like a wrecking ball right before it hits its target. When it hits, he said, "all hell breaks loose." He swings from rage to tears. He is confused and scared at the same time.

Learning the Art of Noticing and Focused Attention

To begin the process for Patrick (and all my clients), I teach them breathing and body-scan exercises. The idea is learning focused attention skills that will help us to control the regulatory circuits of the brain and heighten our awareness, using our five senses. This will help us to alter the explosive flow of energy in our bodies that can derail us at times.

In an earlier chapter, I mentioned that doing a body scan was a helpful way to start noticing where you hold tension in your body. This focused exercise will help train you (and your brain) to slow down and pay attention to what your physical body is experiencing throughout the day. When our bodies are experiencing pain, it is because of an injury of some kind. It can be internal or external. We are wise to pay attention to what our bodies are trying to tell us. This exercise should be done at least twice daily.

Let's begin the art of noticing with learning the practice of doing a body scan. This exercise should take you at least ten minutes. The important thing here is not to rush it. Here's how to begin.

Focusing Exercise 1—Body Scan

Find a comfortable place to sit. Close your eyes. Breathe in, and exhale slowly. Before each body scan, allow yourself a few deep breaths to relax yourself before you begin. Now, start at the top of your head and simply focus your attention there. Take your time with this exercise. Does your head feel heavy? Does it feel light?

Notice your temple area. Does it feel tight? Do you feel any pressure there? Does your head ache?

As you breathe in and out, notice the sensations in your face. Is the face soft? Try to relax your face. Now, notice your nose. Feel the air going in and out of your nostrils. Does it feel warm or cool? Pay attention to how it feels. Pause. Breathe. Next, notice your eyes. Do they feel tired? Sometimes when I'm tired, my eyeballs actually ache in their sockets. Focus your attention on your eyes. Next, move down to your jaws. Do you notice your teeth clenching? I remember noticing this one night as I was doing my scan when I was going to sleep. I had my teeth clenched tight together and my jawbone tense. Notice if your top teeth are touching your bottom ones in a relaxed or tense manner.

Now focus on the back of your head. Is there tension in your neck? Just notice any sensations you may be feeling. Is there tightness, stiffness? Observe those sensations. Be curious about the state of these sensations. What might they be trying to tell you about your body? Stay focused. If you find your mind starting to wander, that's okay. Simply redirect it back to whatever you're observing.

Move down your neck to your shoulders. What do you feel? Does your body feel warm or cool? Stay open-minded throughout this exercise. Move down to your elbows and your forearms. Do you have your arms relaxed? Are your hands folded, or are they lying open next to your body? What do you notice about your hands? Are they warm or cold? Observe those sensations. Are your fingers open or closed? Relaxed or tensed? Keep focusing.

Now move to your chest. Notice your breathing here again. Focus on the rise and fall of your chest in conjunction with the breath. Are you breathing slowly? Are you holding your breath? Sometimes when we are stressed or in pain, we hold our breath.

Do you notice whether your breathing has relaxed you or not? Feel your chest going up and down. Focus all your attention there for a few moments. Then move to your stomach. Often when we are stressed, we'll say we feel as if we have a knot in our stomach. Strong emotions can make us literally feel nauseated, queasy, or tense in the gut. Observe any sensations you're holding in your belly, and make a mental note of why they might be there. No judgments, just noticing.

Next, focus on your spine as you're seated in the chair. Do you feel anything there? Imagine your vertebrae holding up your spinal cord. Focus on any sensations in your back. Does it feel relaxed or tense? Now move to your legs. Focus on how they feel planted firmly on the floor. Move from your thighs down your calves. Do this slowly. What do you notice? Pause. Breathe.

Now focus on your feet. If you're wearing shoes, try wiggling your toes inside your socks. Feel the texture of your socks on your skin. Feel and focus on your feet inside your shoes. Move your feet around a little to feel them grounded on the floor. Notice how they feel. Sore? Tired? No sensation? Finish with a few deep breaths.

Notice if your state is more relaxed now. Make a mental note of which parts of your body are holding the most stress and tightness. Which parts are relaxed? Now, open your eyes.

What do you feel? Has there been a shift in your overall state? Does your body feel more relaxed? If so, how? What made the most difference? Record your insights.

The body scan is a great way to improve your awareness. That's what I want to teach my clients. I want them to observe how they focus their attention. Is it easy to stay focused, or is it hard? Does your mind constantly wander? Or is it easy to stay on point? Are you sidetracked by your thoughts and emotions or memories?

It's okay if you notice you're continually distracted. That doesn't mean you're doing anything wrong. You're just observing your patterns, taking note of how often your mind is tempted to wander. What things distract you? The point of breathing and body-scan exercises is to teach you about your awareness. It's like working out. The more you lift weights, the stronger your muscles become and the easier it is to do. Let's do another exercise.

Focusing Exercise 2—Head, Shoulders, Knees, and Toes

Remember that cute nursery rhyme exercise song your kids sang in pre-school, "Head, Shoulders, Knees, and Toes"? . . . knees and toes? Well, this next exercise is going to get you to focus on your head, shoulders, knees, and toes, or some other body part for one whole minute. For each day, I have a body part listed below, or you can pick your own body part. Let's go! Here is the sample schedule:

Monday: For one minute, focus your attention on your head. When your mind wanders (and we know it will), simply bring your attention back to your head. As you focus on your head, simply think about how it feels sitting on your atlas bone. You can ask yourself: Does it feel light or heavy? Tense or relaxed? No judgments. Just focus and observe. Breathe.

Tuesday: For one minute, focus your attention on your shoulders. When you find your mind wandering, simply guide and direct your gaze back to your shoulders and focus. Did you notice any tension? Breathe.

Wednesday: For an entire minute, focus your attention on the toes of your right foot. Sit quietly and observe them. No judgments, just focused attention. Notice if your mind is wandering any less on day three. There is no right or wrong here. Breathe.

Thursday: Again, focus your attention for one minute on the toes of your left foot. When your mind wanders, direct it back. Pay attention to what you're paying attention to. Focus. Breathe.

Friday: For a minute, pay attention to your knees. Focus on them. Notice any sensations. Think about how you use your knees. When your mind wanders, simply bring it back into focus. Breathe.

Saturday: For yet another minute today, focus your attention on your eyes. You might even open and close them as you sit quietly. What do you notice? What sensations are you aware of in your eyes? If your mind starts to wander, simply bring your eyes back into focus. Breathe.

Sunday: One last time. For one minute, focus your attention on any body part of your choice. When your mind is caught up with other thoughts, feelings, or memories, simply guide your attention back. Observe. Focus and pay attention. Breathe.

Focusing Exercise 3

Sit quietly and bring your hands together so that your palms touch. Gently rub them together and be aware of how the touch and warmth feels. Slowly breathe in and open up your arms out wide. Pause and hold your breath for four counts. Now exhale and bring your palms together again to touch.

Focusing Exercise 4—Attending to Your Breath

Throughout the course of this book, we've talked about relaxation breathing. I'll remind you again that research has proved beyond a shadow of a doubt that the best way to calm an overcharged central nervous system is something we do every moment—breathing. Not just any breathing, but slow, controlled, and intentional breathing. Here's what the American Institute of Stress says about the benefits of deep breathing:

> Abdominal breathing for 20 to 30 minutes each day
> will reduce anxiety and reduce stress. Deep breathing

increases the supply of oxygen to your brain and stimulates the parasympathetic nervous system, which
promotes a state of calmness. Breathing techniques help
you feel connected to your body—it brings your awareness away from the worries in your head and quiets
your mind.[1]

There are different ways to do the breathing. Here are a few you
can try and decide for yourself which is most effective.

Diaphragmatic breathing: Diaphragmatic breathing is also known
as "belly breathing," and it's done by contracting the diaphragm, a
large muscle between the thoracic cavity and the abdominal wall.
As air enters the lungs, the belly expands. It's different than our
normal breathing because it's marked by expansion of the abdo-
men and not the chest. If you've ever watched a sleeping baby, you
may have noticed the rise and fall of the belly, not the chest. To
check your own breathing technique, do this simple self-test.

Check your ability to move the diaphragm by putting your
hands on your body. One hand will go on your stomach (or abdo-
men) and the other on your chest. Try to push out your lower hand
(which is on your belly button) with your abdominal muscles. Can
you breathe using your belly only so that your rib cage and upper
hand do not move?

Now try this: Lie on your back, placing one hand on your
chest. Place a couple of books over your belly button. Close your
eyes and relax your whole body. Breathe in slowly through your
nose. Focus on your breathing and change the way you breathe
so that you can lift the books up about one inch with each inhalation, and then relax to exhale (the books will go down when you
relax to exhale).

Repeat this diaphragmatic breathing exercise for about three-
to-five minutes before your main breathing exercises to reconnect

your conscious brain with the diaphragm. Your book should slowly rise, but your chest should not. When you have taken a full, deep breath, hold it, count to three, then slowly breathe out. Repeat a few times, until your feel relaxed.

For more information, you can go to http://www.normal breathing.com/learn-8-diaphragmatic-breathing.php.[2]

Yogic Breathing 1: There are lots of different yoga breathing exercises. I came across this one called "alternative nostril breathing," and I like it because it really teaches you to focus with the alternate finger movements. It is used to balance the nervous system and help you focus.

To start, make a fist. Now raise your thumb and ring finger up. If you are right-handed, you will be covering your left nostril with your ring finger and your right nostril with your thumb (opposite if you're left-handed). Cover your left nostril with your ring finger and fully exhale. Start the inhalation with the right nostril. Once you've fully inhaled, cover your right nostril. Exhale at the left. Inhale the left, cover the left, exhale at the right. Inhale right. Exhale left.

Now add a retention this time. Inhale right, and when you've taken a full inhalation, close both nostrils, and hold. Release the left and exhale. Inhale left. Close both nostrils, and hold, and exhale right.

Practice this every day. It's a great one to do at night to calm the mind before bed. If you would like more instructions on how to do this, there are several videos available on the *DoYogaWithMe* website.[3]

Yogic Breathing 2: You can do this exercise seated in a comfortable chair with your back upright. Place the tip of your tongue against the back of your front teeth and keep it there through the exercise. You will be exhaling through your mouth around your tongue. First, exhale completely through the mouth. You should make a whoosh sound.

Next, close your mouth and inhale through your nose, counting to four. Hold your breath (to a count of seven).

Now exhale through your mouth (making the whoosh sound) to the count of six. This is going to be a 1:2 breathing practice where you are gradually increasing your exhalation until it's twice as long as your inhalation. This relaxes the nervous system.

Repeat, exhaling through your mouth. Close your mouth and inhale through the nose to a four count. Hold the breath to a seven count. Now, exhale through your mouth to the count of eight. This is a long exhale. Again, the idea is that the exhale should be twice as long as the inhale. Continue for six to eight breaths.

With all these breathing exercises, you may immediately notice a shift in consciousness. You may feel a sense of calm, lightness, detachment, or dreaminess. This is good, because it's telling you that you are calming your involuntary nervous system and diminishing stress. The focusing is helping to increase your awareness. When we talk about prayer, meditation, and contemplation, we will incorporate the breathing into those practices.

The great thing about these exercises is that you can do them anytime and anywhere. You can use them whenever you experience stress or anxiety. You can incorporate them into your exercise program, and I highly recommend that you have such a program, because exercise helps with brain function. It builds endorphins and enkephalins. These are the body's natural painkillers. Enkephalins block pain symptoms in the spinal cord, and endorphins do so principally at the brain stem. These are the body's naturally occurring opiates.

Exploring Mindfulness

The point of all these crazy exercises is the same: *focused attention*. Training your mind. Changing the neuro-networks in your brain. Peace. Well-being. The ability to deal with stress more efficiently. A sense of calm in the midst of life's storms. But it takes work. It takes your making a decision. It takes commitment. Then you will achieve success. Remember, you always have your breath to come back to. Use it!

It would be helpful if you journal your daily moods, exercise regimen, and whether you did or didn't do your focusing exercises. Remember, journaling helps with right- and left-brain integration. But to do this effectively, you will need to write by hand. If you're not used to doing this, it can seem laborious, but it's another skill that will help you focus. We're all so used to typing things out on the computer because it's faster, but the goal here is to slow down. Taking your time. Paying attention. Handwriting in your journal is the optimal way to go.

You may notice that after a few tries at these exercises, you become really frustrated. I know I did, and still do. I am a little on the ADHD side, so sitting still is hard for me, and trying to keep my mind from wandering sometimes seems nearly impossible! Please remember, there is no right or wrong way to do these exercises. If your mind gets sidetracked with thoughts and feelings, it's no big deal. You are in training. Just like an athlete. Keep at it!

This was really hard for Patrick. He noticed that when he tried to do some of the exercises, often he would be overcome with angry emotions. His mind would wander off to his parents and their break-up and how he had been cheated out of a happy family. Patrick realized that staying super-busy was a way he avoided dealing with his feelings about his parent's divorce.

If we're honest, this is the problem for most of us: we do all kinds of things to keep busy so that we can avoid thinking or feeling about the things that we really need to deal with. Distraction is a way we leave ourselves. Whatever defensive strategies we've used, the idea is the same: we build a wall around our awareness so that we don't have to stay present with ourselves and our pain. The truth was that Patrick was angry at his parents about the divorce. The more he tried not to think about it during those quiet times, the more his mind went to that very place. He knew he needed to deal with these troubling emotions, but he was scared.

I asked Patrick if he would be willing to see what these feelings were trying to tell him. In other words, I wanted him to sit with these difficult emotions and learn to be curious instead of judgmental. Sitting with anxiety, sadness, and hurt is not a pleasant thing to do, but it's truly the way to freedom. As much as it hurts, these painful feelings won't kill or destroy us. I know it *feels* as if they will, but as a trauma survivor I can tell you firsthand that they won't.

I told Patrick that learning these skills would teach him how to regulate his mind, and more importantly, how to sit with these uncomfortable emotions *without being overtaken with them*. He agreed to try. I asked him to try not to judge his feelings, but to observe them from a distance. This is the practice of *mindfulness*. What exactly is mindfulness, you might be thinking? It's simply living in the moment. It comes from the English word meaning *awareness*.

It means we become fully present and fully aware of our experience, moment by moment. It also means we have a willingness to receive whatever we experience in the moment, be it positive or negative. It's surrender. We accomplish this awareness without judging, by letting go of evaluations, not drawing conclusions, and not trying to figure everything out! We give it to the Father. This doesn't mean we ignore our feelings; we just notice they're coming up—again. And we choose to simply label them and not get "hooked" into the chaos they create in us.

While mindfulness is usually associated with Eastern religious traditions, we can take some of the principles and exercises and adopt a Christian stance with them. Mindfulness approaches do not have to be bad or evil. In fact, just the opposite is true. One of the things I particularly like about a mindfulness approach is that it calls us to stay in the present moment. For the Christian, living in the moment is the only place to realize Christ as life. If we look to the future, we will experience fear and anxiety with the "what ifs." If we look back at the past, we will experience regrets with the "if onlys."

When Patrick came in to see me again a few weeks after I asked him to continue his mindfulness practices, he was proud to report that he was able to do the assignments successfully. He was able to sit with his feelings and stay present with them nonjudgmentally. He was learning to be still and to be curious about what was really going on in his internal world. This was a really huge step for him. If he could do it once, he knew he could repeat it!

Walking Meditation

While this exercise originates from Buddhist tradition, don't freak out. We are using this exercise to teach a precise awareness of mind and body. This is *not* emptying the mind or anything like that. You are simply learning to focus and become aware.

Walking meditation develops balance and accuracy of awareness as well as durability of concentration. Here is an example of how to begin. Map out a path to begin your walk. Thirty paces are fine to start. The idea is to notice the lifting, moving, and placing of each foot. In each case, you must try to keep your mind on just the sensations of walking.

Stand at one end of the path and focus your mind on the sensations of the body. First, let the attention rest on the feeling of the body standing upright, with the arms hanging naturally and the hands lightly clasped in front or behind. Allow the eyes to gaze at a point about a foot in front of you at ground level, thus avoiding visual distraction. Now, walk gently, at a deliberate but "normal" pace, to the end of the path. Stop. Focus on the body, standing for the period of a couple of breaths. Turn, and walk back again. While walking, be aware of the general flow of physical sensations, or more closely direct your attention to the feet. The exercise for the mind is to keep bringing its attention back to the sensation of the feet touching the ground, the spaces between each step, and the feelings of stopping and starting.

Of course, the mind will wander, so it is important to cultivate patience, and the resolve to begin again. Adjust the pace to suit your state of mind—vigorous when you're drowsy or trapped in obsessive thought, firm but gentle when you're restless and impatient. At the end of the path, stop; breathe in and out; "let go" of any restlessness, worry, bliss, memories, or opinions about yourself. The "inner chatter" may stop momentarily or fade out. Begin again. In this way, you continually refresh the mind and allow it to settle at its own rate.

Walking brings energy and fluidity into the practice, so keep your pace steady and just let whatever feelings or thoughts you notice pass through your mind. It is natural for our untrained minds to become absorbed in thought. Instead of giving in to impatience, learn how to let go, and begin again. Remember, it's like working a muscle—you have to keep at it to get stronger.

Patrick was practicing these exercises daily at home. I was really excited because many clients don't do their daily homework, so their progress is impaired. In one of our sessions, he shared that while he was doing the exercises, he would have recurring thoughts of worthlessness. Thoughts such as, "You're a loser," "You can't do anything right," and "You'll never get anywhere in life because something's wrong with you." These thoughts kept coming up, and they plagued him. I told him this was the voice of the Judger—his critical sub-personality that was trying to thwart his progress.

In these moments, Patrick needed something more than just a new strategy to convince himself that what his mind was offering up to him were lies, or that his feelings weren't real. We can't change how we feel by simply telling ourselves to feel differently. If we could, no one would be unhappy or stressed out. Cultivating awareness helps us give time to honor the thoughts and feelings we are experiencing and to accept them but not allow ourselves to be overtaken by them. Spending inordinate amounts of energy fighting against thoughts and feelings is unproductive. It doesn't work anyway because, as we've seen, the more we try not to think of something, the more we do! Instead, accept what is, and see what happens.

I asked Patrick if there was a kinder way he could communicate to himself. Instead of saying, "You can't do anything right," could he try something like, "I'm frustrated at myself right now because I haven't done my best, but there are lots of things I do well"? I also asked Patrick to write down three of his positive attributes and one positive thing someone who knew him might say about him.

Finally, I asked him to come up with a special resource person, someone who was safe and trustworthy. When he felt down on himself, I asked him to imagine this resource person telling him what he needed to hear. What would this person say about him? Would he be willing to receive that from this person? Could he access this person regularly as a support? If he couldn't come up with anyone, I asked him to imagine what I might say to him during these difficult moments and to reflect on those thoughts.

Building a Safe, Peaceful Place

One other exercise I gave Patrick to do for homework was to create a safe and tranquil place in his mind that he could access when anxiety, fear, depression, or anger overwhelmed him. To help him get started with this exercise, I asked him to consider the following questions while writing his script:

- Where would be the most peaceful, relaxing, beautiful place to go to in all the world?
- What does this place look like?
- What are you doing in this place?
- Who is with you?
- Is this place warm or cold?
- How would you describe it to someone who has never been there?
- Is it quiet or noisy?
- What smells do you notice?
- What sensations do you feel on your skin, if any?
- What sights and sounds do you notice there?
- What textures?
- What does the sky look like?
- Describe the sun, the moon, the stars.
- How do you feel being there?
- Why is this place safe and special?

What I was asking Patrick (and I ask all my clients) to do when practicing focused reflection is to draw a vivid mental picture of a safe, tranquil place. It's important that this be done with great detail to help with concentration and focus. This is a self-directed intellectual and visual process that engages different parts of the brain. It helps with emotional regulation, body regulation, uncontrolled anger, and thought calming. When you do this exercise, to make it more integrative for your brain, I'd like you to write out this script as you picture it in your mind.

Writing engages the basil ganglion (remember that little group of structures from Chapter Two), the cerebellum (these work together to fine-tune movement), and the motor cortex (where nerve impulses initiate voluntary muscle activity). Remember, the basil ganglion are responsible for helping to turn thought into action. This structure also helps integrate feelings with movement. It can calm or accelerate motor behavior. I know that when my grief was especially overwhelming, I would start to write my feelings down sometimes in utter hysteria, only to find calm as my pen flew through the pages of my journal.

Research on the cerebellum confirms that this structure not only helps with the development and management of gross motor skills, such as running and skipping, but with brain integration as well. "Furthermore, Rand Nelson of Peterson Directed Handwriting believes that when children are exposed to cursive handwriting, *changes occur in their brains* that allow a child to overcome motor challenges" (italics mine).[4] That is, cursive writing ability affords us the opportunity to naturally train these fine motor skills by taking advantage of a child's inability to fully control his fingers. This means cursive writing acts as a building block rather than as a stressor, providing a less strenuous learning experience; "moreover, cursive handwriting stimulates brain synapses and synchronicity between the left and right hemispheres, something absent from printing, typing or keyboarding."[5]

Dr. Leaf says this on how writing helps with brain integration:

This method of pouring out your thoughts [through writing] encourages *both sides of the brain* to work

together to integrate the two perspectives of thought—
the left side of the brain looks at information from the
detail to the big picture and the right side of the brain
from the big picture to the detail. For full understanding to take place—which will result in the conversion
of short-term memory to long-term memory—both
perspectives of thought need to come together.[6]
(italics mine)

Here is an example of how to construct a safe, peaceful place.
This was a very meaningful exercise to me because God used
the image of the Lion (Aslan in *The Chronicles of Narnia*, and
Jesus the Lion of Judah) in my healing work (I did a lot of Eye
Movement Desensitization Reprocessing—EMDR). To this day,
the lion shows up everywhere to remind me that Jesus is with me
and he will never leave me. This is a source of tremendous peace.
My safe-place script looked like this:

I see myself; I am walking on a path in the forest alone.
I notice the pathway feels soft beneath my feet. As I
look down, I observe the soil, leaves, twigs, rocks, and
the gnarly roots of the grand trees under my feet. I am
aware of my breath. I breathe in through my nose to
fill my lungs. I exhale slowly. Again, I breathe in to the
count of four, hold it to the count of seven, exhale to the
count of eight. I repeat this several times to relax.

As I walk through the forest, I notice the smell of
the trees. It's fresh, clean. I smell the tall pines. I notice
the texture of the bark on the trees. I stop to run my
hands over the bark, paying attention to how it looks
and feels against my hands. I look to my left and I
notice the lake. It's calm. The water is very still. I pause.
I notice I'm having sad thoughts. I make no judgments.

THINK THIS NOT THAT

I just observe. I bring my mind back to my breath. The sky is clear. I notice the different shades of blue as well as the white fluffy clouds.

I am waiting for him to come. He always does. Looking around, I notice some rocks. The sun is shining down on me, and I feel the warmth on my skin. It bathes my entire being. It feels so relaxing. I hear the sounds of the forest. The birds. The rustling of leaves in the distance. I notice that my mind starts to wander. Sad thoughts again. I notice and name them. I realize they will come and go. I let them float by as if they were on a cloud. I try to refocus my attention on the breath.

As I round the corner, I see him in the distance. There is a deep sense of elation in my spirit. Somehow, he is beside me, and we are walking together. It's Aslan. The Lion. He is there with me just like before. He has always been with me. He was there that fateful day. He was there caring for me. I reach down and I touch his mane. It's so soft. He turns his head and looks up at me. His eyes are like fire piercing my soul. I have never felt such peace. He will never leave me. Never hurt me. Never disappoint me. He is safe. Even to my old age and gray hairs, he will care for me and sustain me.

I walk slowly with him, my hands holding on to the fur in his mane. I notice it's the color of honey. I feel it between my fingers. The texture is coarse but, at the same time, soft. He feels warm. There is an earthen smell surrounding him. He walked with me through the tragedy. He was angry. He stood up on his hind legs and roared. It filled the room. He knows I'm sad. He knows how much my heart has been shattered. He knows my soul. Once again, he roars as if to say he understands.

We walk together through the woods. I love the tall trees and how they shade the dirt path. I don't have to speak. I'm just experiencing the presence of the One who restores my soul. In a moment, he is gone. I'm alone, but not really. His presence has filled me once again. I close and open my eyes and reawaken. I breathe deeply. The feeling of peace and calm surrounds me.

How did it feel reading this? If you think this might be a helpful exercise, jump in and write your own script. It's not about right or wrong here. This is *your* safe and peaceful place. Make it what you want. Just remember to pay attention to your breath as you're doing this, and make it detailed so that you are including lots of things for your mind to focus on to increase your sensory awareness. When anxiety, stress, anger, or depression overwhelm you—go to this place in your mind. Just a few minutes of daily practice can make a tremendous difference. Don't forget, if your mind wanders, it's okay.

Keys to Practicing Awareness—Observing, Describing, and Participating

Observation is the first key factor in cultivating awareness and creating a gentle shift in consciousness. At the beginning of this book, we talked about observing. Now, equipped with these new focusing techniques, see how much deeper you can go with this. This is important because when we're in pain, when we're suffering, and when we're having toxic thoughts about the situations and events in our lives, rather than leaving ourselves when things become unpleasant (through our old coping strategies), observing helps us stay present with our pain and not run from it. Think of it as self-monitoring of body, mind, and spirit.

When we're highly aroused, this is a great exercise to help us calm down and focus. I use this all the time with my clients, and it's so amazing to be able to see the shift they make by doing it in my office. First, I ask them to take a couple of deep breaths to focus. Then I ask them to look around the room and identify three objects that they find pleasant and name them out loud.

When they're done, I ask them to focus on one of those objects and begin to describe it (the second part of being mindful). I then ask them to tell me why this object is particularly pleasant to them. Over and over, I am amazed at how their countenance changes. Sometimes a little smile will come over their face, as a peaceful and pleasant memory comes to mind. Finally, I ask them to participate in some way with the object. If it's the huge aloe plant I have in the room, they may go over and touch it. If it's the pretty teal blue pillow with tons of folds on it, they may want to hold it.

What I'm wanting to teach them is that they have the power to hold both the unpleasant (remember, when they come in they are in high arousal) and the pleasant. The exercise is helping them make the shift from the unpleasant feelings they are experiencing to what is pleasant in their surroundings. When we're struggling, we view our state of being as an either/or situation. Either things are good, or they are bad. I want them to see that it can be "the-and-both" and show them that they can hold both—the good and the bad—and still be okay.

When Thoughts Get Fused Together

Madison is a great example of someone who ran from pain. She came to my office because she had spent years using food as a way to numb herself and avoid difficult emotions. Madison's eating disorder had become not only a way of life for her, but her entire identity. She was "cognitively fused" to her thinking, meaning her thoughts had become so embedded in her mind, her mental evaluations, and her life story (not to mention her vocabulary and thought-life) that she couldn't see anything outside of her eating-disorder world.

What exactly is cognitive fusion, and why is it so important to be aware of it in our thought-life?

Acceptance and Commitment Therapy (ACT) offers summaries to help you recognize and distinguish Cognitive Fusion and Cognitive Defusion.[7] Below, I have charted the ACT summaries alongside how Madison experienced them.

Cognitive Fusion	Madison's Experience
"A thought is a mental construction (largely verbally construed) that can really, really seem like . . . something that is actually real and something that masquerades as . . . the absolute truth."	To Madison, the thought and the image of "fat" were the absolute truth to her, even though the words and images didn't resemble her at all. She wouldn't consider otherwise.
"A command you have to obey or a rule you must follow."	Madison's eating-disorder voice became her identity and her god.
"The past, or the historical reality of your conditioned/learned experience."	Madison's mom repeatedly said she was fat.
"You may be mindlessly fused to your mind's predictions and fabrications of your entirely dreamed up and vividly imagined future."	Madison believed she would be an old maid if she was fat.
"Some critical perspective so very important that it requires all your attention."	Madison made negative attributions about herself and ruminated on them endlessly.
"Some idea or conclusion that you won't let go of, even if it worsens your life."	Madison would not let go of her already established conclusions, even though they were making her life miserable.

To help Madison defuse these thoughts I gave her this list:

Cognitive Defusion	Madison's Experience
"You can see a thought for what it is: nothing more or less than a bunch of words or pictures 'inside your head.' In a state of de-fusion, you recognize that a thought may or may not be true."	Madison could now consider that her thoughts were not bearers of truth, that they were simply thoughts.
"You can see that a thought is definitely not a command you have to obey or a rule you have to follow, definitely not a threat to you."	Madison did not have to listen to the eating disorder's voice. She had the power to choose for herself.
"You can see that a thought is not something happening in the physical world—it's merely words or pictures inside your head."	Madison's mental picture of "fat" was constructed from her mother's words.
"You can see that a thought may or may not be important—you have a choice as to how much you believe (ACT calls this 'believability' our own mind's judgments and interpretations)."	Madison could choose to modify or change her existing thoughts/beliefs.
"You can see that a thought can be allowed to come and go of its own accord without any need for you to hold on, control the experience, or repress, deny, or attempt to push it away."	I taught Madison to simply observe that she was having a thought that she was fat—but make no judgment.

Madison tried hard to dismiss, avoid, or ignore her negative thoughts, but they continued to torment her. I told her to just let them come and to simply observe them while taking a non-judgmental stance. The next time Madison told herself she was a fat slob, I had her say out loud, "I guess I'm accepting the thought that I'm a fat slob again." Every time she had this thought, she was to say it out loud. She counted fifty times in one day.

When we are fused to our thoughts, we can't observe them objectively. Remember in Chapter Six that we talked about the explanatory style of "Me Always Me"? With that style of thinking, we are cognitively fused to a thought or to a pattern of thinking that leaves no room for anyone else to have contributed to a problem or situation. Madison couldn't separate the "ED voice" from her true identity. She felt she had to obey this voice because *she* was the problem.

Once she learned to practice cognitive de-fusion, it helped her see that the ED voice was the problem. It was robbing her of her true identity. She was able to move to a "me not always me" explanatory style of thinking and make room for a more objective view of things. Being objective with toxic thoughts is crucial if we don't want to give them power over us.

As time went on, Madison learned to do this quite well. She was able to notice her inner self-critic and be kinder to herself. She was able to see that this ED voice was actually an imposter she had created to meet her needs for adequacy and value. In time, it had taken over her authentic self. By practicing cognitive de-fusion, she was able to reclaim her true identity, modify set-in-stone beliefs, and start the rewiring process.

Recapping Mindfulness Skills

As we've seen, mindfulness practice has three key ingredients: *observing, describing,* and *participation.* The exercises we've gone through include all three of these core elements. Remember not to get ahead of yourself. First, observe. Be a noticer of your body and the sensations it holds. Describing includes labeling what you observe. Muscles feel tense, stomach feels sick, neck aches. You're really doing a little bit of all this in these exercises.

The key is that you want to tease apart the feelings, interpretations, and meanings you have assigned to events that are troubling you and see if you can stick with the facts. For example: when I'm feeling guilt about what I should have done with Mike, I can say,

"The truth is that he is not here anymore. I did my best to help him, and now I have to move forward." Or if I'm putting words to the experience, I could say, "Guilt is taking over me again." Or if I'm labeling what I observe, I can say, "I'm having sad and guilty thoughts." I'm trying not to attach meaning to it now but to trust God with what I couldn't control.

The next piece is participating. This means you stay in the present moment. You don't avoid or suppress your feelings, and you don't run away from them. People who experience grief over the loss of a loved one recover more quickly if they work through their pain. This may include crying, screaming, writing, talking, being quiet. Participating requires a willingness to accept what we can't change and to engage in the experience we find ourselves in adaptively.

For example, if I'm stuck in traffic, I can gripe and moan and be sour, or I can accept it and participate in the experience of having to wait by deciding to listen to a tape, a radio show, or some music, and try to enjoy it instead of focusing on how sour I am that I'm in the situation.

In the next chapter, we are going to look at how to specifically redesign our thoughts for optimum health and well-being.

NOTES

[1]Kellie Marksberry, "Take a Deep Breath," The American Institute of Stress, August 10, 2012, http://www.stress.org/take-a-deep-breath/.

[2]"Diaphragmatic Breathing: Techniques and Instructions," NormalBreathing .com, accessed March 17, 2017, http://www.normalbreathing.com/learn-8 -diaphragmatic-breathing.php.

[3]"Yoga Breathing Exercises: Pranayama Videos," Do Yoga With Me, accessed March 15, 2017, https://www.doyogawithme.com/yoga_breathing.

[4]David Sortino, "Brain Research and Cursive Writing," The Press Democrat, May 22, 2013, http://davidsortino.blogs.pressdemocrat.com/10221/brain -research-and-cursive-writing/.

[5]Sortino, "Brain Research and Cursive Writing."

[6]Leaf, *Switch on Your Brain*.

[7]"Hands Entangled De-Fusion Metaphor" (PDF), online supplement to "Hart Center Intake Forms and Extra Fancy Exercises and Articles," The Hart Center, https://www.thehartcenter.com/wp-content/uploads/2011/11/Hands -De-Fusion-Metaphor-.pdf.

Chapter Eleven

REPROGRAMING YOUR MIND: REDESIGNING YOUR THOUGHTS

As the deer pants for streams of water,
 so my soul pants for you, my God.
My soul thirsts for God, for the living God.
 When can I go and meet with God.

—Psalm 42:1–2

My thoughts trouble me and I am distraught.

—Psalm 55:2

Who of you by worrying can add a single hour to your life?

—Luke 12:25

The whole focus of this book has been about what to do with troubling thoughts. Thoughts that distress us. Thoughts that are toxic. Thoughts that cause us more harm than we even realize. Thoughts that take us away from connecting to our true power source, the Holy Spirit.

Toxic thoughts are really like a virus that infects your computer. If you've ever had one, you know it can destroy your machine or wreak enough havoc to make your life miserable. That's why we have to eradicate toxic thinking and, in its place, redesign our thoughts to reflect the mind of Christ.

In Chapter Four, we looked at how to develop positive counterstatements to replace negative attributions. This was called reframing. Reframing is key, and now you understand how the task of writing out your reframes benefits your brain. Remember that for all this to work, you need to have some degree of belief that the thoughts, counterstatements, changes, or modifications that you make to your set-in-stone beliefs can be true.

To strengthen the neurocircuitry in these newly adopted thoughts, you have to meditate, ponder, reflect, and think on them over and over. Just as you've spent hours upon hours ruminating about the negative, you have to do the same thing while dwelling on the positive. You do this through understanding, participating, and practicing the exercises we've learned in this book.

The Power of Reflection

In Chapter Four, we also looked at the Four Rs: *Recognize, Refute,* and *Reframe,* which will lead to the *Rewiring* of our neuropathways. Those are key elements to this practice. I want to add one more "R" to your practice now, and that's the word *Reflect.* Reflection will incorporate all the mindfulness practices we've talked about so far, and it will be a nice segue into our final and most powerful weapon of change—connecting to the heart of God through the practice of the spiritual disciplines.

If you've been tracking with me this far and doing the exercises, you should be getting used to being still and focusing your mind. We've talked a lot about noticing, awareness, and consciousness, and now we want to explore the idea of *focused reflection.* You may be wondering why I keep beating these concepts to death (although hopefully by now you're convinced there is plenty of merit in them), but consider this: how have you approached the skills you've learned so far in this book? Are you simply absorbing facts as you're reading, or do you want to take these principles, tools, and skills and *experience* something life-changing for yourself?

The answer to that question will help define everything else in your life and in your brain. In fact, take a moment now, put the book down, and really consider the answer to that question. There is no right or wrong answer, just an honest assessment of where you are currently and where you want to go.

It should come as no surprise that most of us are moving at such a fast pace in our daily lives that we have little or no time for reflection. This wasn't true in the days when Augustine, Calvin, Wesley, and Merton were writing about the "inner devotional life." These practices were second nature to them. They took their faith seriously. They prayed, fasted, and pursued meditaion. The disciplines were a way of life for them, just like cell phones, Internet, and YouTube are a way of life for us now.

As I read the works of these saints, one thing I notice is that each of them had a deep longing to experience God. In many ways, that's missing for us in today's culture. Maybe it's because we have so much that we don't feel like we need as much of God. It's important to note that practicing the spiritual disciplines wasn't something done out of duty. They weren't laws to be obeyed. They weren't done from a legalistic viewpoint. They weren't self-improvement oriented. They were done with one motive—having a deep experiential connection to God. My friend Henry Blackaby brought this idea to bear in his book entitled *Experiencing God: Knowing and Doing the Will of God.*

In order to experience changing your thoughts (and all the neurobiology behind that), in order to experience a change of any kind, you have to begin by reflecting on your inner world. You have to long, as the deer who pants after the water, to be transformed. If you look at Scripture, you'll find that Jesus, along with many of the heroes of our faith, withdrew to a quiet place to reflect, meditate, pray, contemplate, and listen to his Father. Why? Because he knew it would *renew, refresh, restore, and reequip* him for the battles that lay ahead. As we add this fifth "R" (Reflect) to our list, here are some questions to ponder:

> Do I desire to grow and change both emotionally
>   and spiritually?
> What obstacles might stand in the way of change?
> How can I carve out pockets of time in my day
>   for reflection?
> Who am I, and who is God?
> What are my core values? Have they changed over time?
>   Why?
> What occupies my thought-life?
> At this time, how willing am I to work on changing
>   my thoughts?
> Am I satisfied with my life? What changes do I want to
>   make moving forward?
> What are my goals for the future?
> What am I passionate about?
> What did I learn about myself from my life experiences?
> What fears do I have about embarking on a spiritual
>   journey with God?
> What areas in my life do I need to experience more
>   freedom in?

As we embark on this spiritual journey, keep in mind it is just that, a journey, not a race. Transformation is a process. It's about slow and constant changes—changes that you and everyone around you will ultimately notice. It won't be your own strength. It won't be your own work. It won't be willpower. It will be the deep work of the Holy Spirit. I have seen this in my own life as I've sought the heart of God, yielding myself to him, entreating him for help in the darkest nights of the soul that anyone can imagine. I found God through these practices, and in the process, I took a terribly traumatized brain and found some healing. I believe you can do the same.

People marveled at how on earth I ever could have returned to our bedroom where I found Mike shot to death in the bed, not to mention how I could ever sleep in there again. How could I find peace there? How could I stop seeing those horrific images? There is only one answer for something like that: Jesus. He showed up. He got me back into the bedroom. He broke through the horror and replaced it with his peace.

Here's how it happened. I was sitting outside the closed door of the bedroom, because for the first months I couldn't bear to look in. Just looking would trigger a PTSD event. The door remained shut for a couple months while renovations took place. One day I was alone in the house, only for a half hour or so. Somehow, I found myself outside that room. I had my Bible in my lap, and I was rocking back and forth outside the door. I opened the Bible, and God gave me the verse in 1 Corinthians: "My grace is sufficient for thee, for my power is made perfect in weakness."

I began to reflect on this. My utter weakness. My complete brokenness. My despair at losing my beloved husband in such a ghastly way. I then recalled another time in the past when God used this same verse in my life—when my mom was in the hospital with lung cancer. It gave me strength. It gave me courage. Somehow, this process of reflection gave me new strength, and before I knew it, I was inside the room, weeping on the floor. I came into conscious awareness when my sister-in-law Tori was suddenly at my side praying with me.

Your relationship with God will speak volumes about where your thought-life is focused. That doesn't mean you won't get off-track, but you will be seriously grounded in truth and nothing will be able to move you. Only the Holy Spirit can place the longing inside your heart and move you toward change. Take time each day; practice reflection. Not only will it help you know yourself, it will help you know others, and that will increase your capacity for empathy.

Self-Reflection and Emotional Regulation

Go back to the Dysfunctional Thought Record you created in Chapter Nine. Hopefully you have been keeping a log of situations that have caused you dysfunctional thoughts. This is critical. You have to make these links in your mind in order to change. I'll say it again: you can't change what you don't notice.

You may have been doing this exercise by simply going through the motions. That's okay. But now it's time to really reflect on some of the scenarios you've recorded. That's going to have a different feel. My example is recorded at the beginning of Chapter Nine, and I'm going to walk you through my traumatic memories to show you how to reflect instead of just recording the information. Here is a list of facts about what was going on for me. My reflections follow.

SITUATION	BELIEFS
Mike's suicide	It's my fault.
	I should have died with him.
THOUGHTS	I can't go on living without Mike.
It's my fault.	I'm going to die.
I should have flown back with him that day, and this wouldn't have happened.	I have nothing.
I'm going to kill myself to end this pain.	I will never get over this.
I won't ever make it through this.	

FEELINGS	GOALS/FLESH STRATEGIES
Horror	Avoid the pain
Panic	Dissociate
Fear	Anxiety
Insecurity	Be depressed
Confusion	Be helpless
Guilt	Be co-dependent
Shame	
Abandonment	**COGNITIVE DISTORTIONS**

PAST	COGNITIVE DISTORTIONS
He tried this before several times.	Jumping to conclusions
He was out of control.	Mind reading
I was a mess.	Personalizing
I was disoriented.	Negative self-defeating thinking
	Should, musts, have-tos, and oughts
FEAR	Catastrophizing
I should have predicted he would really do it. I'm a therapist.	Emotional reasoning
Mike will abandon me.	

There you have it. Here is how I went about tackling this as time went on. First, I had to (R) Recall the trauma. I had to do this over and over with my therapist. It was hell. Recollection gave way to self-reflection, where I was able to see and observe other parts of myself besides the ones that were screaming guilt and shame at me.

I was able to be curious about the compassionate part of myself and begin to show myself grace and mercy. This took time. Reflection also opened up room for God to come in and work. Recalling what I knew about God and how he had worked in my life before, I was able to bring that into the present and receive from him.

I had some amazing visions of Jesus holding me, Jesus and me in a boat with a storm raging around us (the storm represented the tormenting thoughts) and Jesus holding up his hand against them as if he was saying, "Stop." He held me tightly under his cloak to protect me. I may have mentioned before that the first vision God gave me to replace the horror of what I walked into that afternoon in our bedroom was of a huge cross on the bed in front of Mike and Jesus hovering above him with his hands outstretched. It was Jesus's blood pouring out over Mike for his salvation. That was powerful!

The Reframing occurred in several ways for me. Through reflection and visual reframing, I was able to work through the trauma, but this time taking my safe place with me (Aslan from the previous chapter). Recalling that fateful day, I walked up the stairs and relived that event while holding on to his mane.

As I recalled the event, I was able to reflect on the fact that Jesus, in the form of the Lion, was not only with me but was sensitive to my pain and horror in that moment. As I previously mentioned, before this, I only thought of how horrible it was for Mike in those last lonely hours or moments. I was undone by that. Now, I could enlarge my capacity to embrace my own pain and despair.

Journaling all this gave me the opportunity to integrate my right/left brain as well as being able to evaluate the toxic thought and write out scriptural counterstatements. By focused reflection, reframing, and the other components, I was able to change my underlying neuronal networks and begin building new healthy thoughts. Each time a toxic thought came into my mind, I had to take it captive. This wasn't a quick fix. It's taken years because of the nature of the trauma. But now, when I have a flashback, my brain defaults to the images I explained above. I have greater emotion regulation. There are new neuropathways now!

Facing Your Dragons

I had to be willing to walk head-on into this agony. There was no avoiding it if I wanted to move forward. I did things such as getting back to sleeping in our bedroom alone (someone slept with me for the first couple months). Driving again (this took five or six months). I resumed watching TV again (I was terrified by the sound of a gunshot or seeing blood). I began going out. I looked at Mike's picture. I got on an airplane, first with my daughter, and finally a year or so later, alone (these were all major PTSD triggers for me, first, because my husband flew his own plane, and second, because I flew home to Washington Reagan before I found Mike). In time, I was able to go back to the airport by myself. As I finish this chapter, I just went back to his dental office for the first time in twenty-eight months. It was so hard to do, and I was a mess, but I did it.

The other thing I did was examine my explanatory styles. Using the models given by Reivich and Shatté, I was able to really make some headway. The guilt I carried for the first year was unexplainable. It was unimaginable. I thought it would kill me, and I truly despaired of life because of it. But focusing on my explanatory style of "me not always me" helped me to reflect and see that I wasn't the only contributor to the suicide. My personality and my coping strategies dispose me to a "me always me" explanatory style, but I had to be willing to broaden my lens as I looked at this tragedy.

Mike refused help. He was always the hero, and it's hard for heroes to accept weakness or to ask for help. On the front end of his situation, he made some poor choices that contributed to his death. I had to accept that. Everyone around me told me I had been a good wife to Mike through the years. But I wasn't about to buy into that. I was to blame. Period. The more I ruminated and thought on these toxic thoughts, the more protein synthesis occurred and the more the toxic pathways were strengthened. These internal battles I was having with myself and with God were throwing my entire system off-balance and disconnecting me from the parts of myself that needed compassion and healing.

Dr. Leaf explains the neurochemistry of this:

> The branches with all the memories and emotions are attached to a cell body with a type of protein that is like glue—like branches attached to a tree trunk. There is more glue on the branches that are used the most, so when you shift your attention from the negative, toxic thought to the positive, healthy, new replacement thought, three things happen.[1]

These three things can be summarized as follows:

- The toxic thoughts become weaker.
- Neurochemicals are produced—chemicals like oxytocin, which remolds; dopamine, which increases focus; and serotonin, which makes you feel good, are released, weakening toxic thoughts.
- This "glue" starts moving away from the toxic tree to a healthy tree.

Reflection and the Inward Disciplines of the Spirit

In Chapter Three, we looked at all the things in our culture that "hook" us into a fast-paced, instant-gratification lifestyle—things that vie for our attention and keep us distracted. In our culture, we can be guaranteed three things: busyness, stress, and noise. In fact, the Enemy of our soul delights in these distractions because they keep peace, stillness, and quiet at bay. He uses temptation, condemnation, and deception to gain ground in our minds. If we aren't busy, there must be something wrong with us!

Here's how I see it. The Enemy tempts us to keep busy, because when we're busy and distracted (with FB, Internet, iPhone, whatever), we're tempted to avoid feeling our pain. For my eating-disordered clients, it's as simple as being distracted with food to find comfort from the emptiness inside. The problem is that after the binge, purge, or food restriction, they're still empty. Then the Enemy comes back and condemns them for their behavior. The worst thing, however, is that he deceives them into thinking they're bad. Not that the behavior was bad, but that *they are* (intrinsically) bad (emotional reasoning).

What do we do with all this? How can all we've learned and practiced so far help us to solidify changes in our brain that will last? Glad you asked. Learning skills is great. We need them. But focusing on your knees and toes isn't enough. You need to put your focus where you will find real truth—in Christ. He is the game-changer. He is the only one who can convince you of your intrinsic worth apart from your performance. That's why I love the disciplines of the Spirit; they connect us to the heart of the Father. I can tell my clients all day long how adequate, secure, acceptable, loved, and valued they are, but when God speaks that into their hearts—boom! It's in cement. It isn't going anywhere.

As I said earlier, neurons that fire together wire together, according to Hebb's Law. Well, there isn't any better way to actively engage that firing process than by focusing and reflecting on the truth of your identity in Christ. That's where the magic happens. That's where real and lasting change occurs, because you aren't just pulling some statement out of your hat, trying to convince yourself to believe it.

So let me introduce you to the inward disciplines of the Spirit. The first one is meditation. This is going to require that we use some of the skills we've already learned, such as silence and soli-tude. I know, I can feel your pain, but if you've been doing the exercises along the way, you've already been practicing this. If you're not convinced that meditation can and will change your brain, here's some research to support this.

- "In a study published in the journal *NeuroImage* in 2009, [Eileen Luders] and her colleagues at University of California Los Angeles School of Medicine] compared the brains of 22 meditators and 22 age-matched non-meditators and found that the meditators (who practiced a wide range of traditions and had between 5 and 46 years of meditation experience) had more gray matter in regions of the brain that are important for attention, emotion regulation, and mental flexibility."[2]
- "MRI scans show that after an eight-week course of mindfulness practice, the brain's 'fight or flight' center, the amygdala, appears to shrink. This primal region of the brain, associated with fear and emotion, is involved in the initiation of the body's response to stress. As the amygdala shrinks, the pre-frontal cortex—associated with higher order brain functions such as awareness, concentration and decision-making—becomes thicker. The "functional connectivity" between these regions—i.e., how often they are activated together—also changes. The connection between the amygdala and the rest of the brain gets weaker, while the connections between areas associated with attention and concentration get stronger."[3]
- "Sue McGreevey of Massachusetts General Hospital writes: 'Previous studies from Sara Lazar's group and others found structural differences between the brains of experienced meditation practitioners and individuals with no history of meditation, observing thickening of the cerebral cortex in areas associated with attention and emotional integration. But those investigations

could not document that those differences were actually produced by meditation.' Until now, that is. The participants spent an average of 27 minutes per day practicing mindfulness exercises, and this is all it took to stimulate a major increase in gray matter density in the hippocampus, the part of the brain associated with self-awareness, compassion, and introspection. McGreevey adds: 'Participant-reported reductions in stress also were correlated with decreased gray-matter density in the amygdala, which is known to play an important role in anxiety and stress. None of these changes were seen in the control group, indicating that they had not resulted merely from the passage of time.'"[4]

Meditation is something we learn from practicing. I can provide a few suggestions, but Nike hit the nail on the head here—you have to *Just do it!* Just as you approached the body scan, the grounding work, and the other exercises we covered, this one begins with finding a comfortable space to reflect and contemplate. Sitting is probably best, otherwise you might fall asleep. Some people like setting aside a specific time to meditate; others just carve it into their day when they have time.

While there are many things to meditate on, I like to focus on a passage of Scripture. When I give this assignment to clients, I ask that they take one week to meditate and reflect on a specific verse, asking God to personalize it into their lives. The idea is that the written Word becomes alive and speaks something into your life and your experience in the here and now. One important caveat: Christian meditation is not emptying the mind. It's filling the mind with Christ's presence. It's not detaching from everything. It's realizing your attachment to the ultimate attachment figure—God.

Suppose, for example, I chose to meditate on the passage in Philippians 4 that says, "The Lord is near." I want to reflect on how my current life-state (let's say I'm having anxiety) would be different if I could truly appropriate the nearness of God. If I really believe the Lord is near, how anxious should I be? How can believing and meditating on his nearness calm my spirit? How do I experience his nearness? What does it look and feel like? Using the Four Rs, I now enter recollection; I recall past experiences of God's nearness and how they affected me. I recall times when his nearness moved me out of an anxious state and into a state of peaceful trust.

Recollection is an important part of meditation. Isaiah 26:3 says, "You will keep in *perfect peace* those whose minds are steadfast because they trust in you" (italics mine). This is a beautiful verse that suggests that if we reflect and recall the things the Lord has done for us, we can apply those truths to any current difficulty we are facing and be confident the Lord will bring us peace.

Practicing reflection and meditation gives you the opportunity also to incorporate other disciplines like prayer or fasting. You can also incorporate a time for "walking meditation" as you reflect on a passage of Scripture. Instead of focusing on your footsteps, legs, or feet, try to focus on nature and glorify God as you walk. Psalm 46:10 provides a nice segue into thinking about how we can glorify God, the Creator. (Focus on that verse: "Be still, and know that I am God; I will be exalted among the nations, I will be exalted in the earth.")

I know I sound like a broken record, but remember, when you're doing your time of meditation and reflection and your mind wanders, bring it back. This is training and exercising your brain! Here's what Michele Rosenthal says in an article from *RewireMe*:

The process of meditation is a terrific strategy for training your brain in the area of attention because it deliberately creates neural pathways dedicated to deliberate control of your focus. Studies have shown that in as little as five minutes per day over a period of just ten weeks, meditation can significantly increase prefrontal activity and strength, resulting in a quieting of your overall mind and specific lower brain structures. The myth about meditation is that you have to empty your mind in order for it to be successful. In fact, your mind *must* wander in order for meditation to have the desired training effect.[5]

Here's what Andrew Newberg and Mark Robert Waldman say about meditation in their book, *How God Changes Your Brain:*

Activities involving meditation and intensive prayer permanently strengthen neural functioning in specific parts of the brain that are involved with lowering anxiety and depression, enhancing social awareness and empathy, and improving cognitive and intellectual functioning.[6]

Newberg and Waldman also say:

If you stay in a contemplative state for twenty minutes to an hour, your experiences will tend to feel more real, affecting your nervous system in ways that enhance physical and emotional health. Anti-stress hormones and neurochemicals are released throughout the body, as well as pleasure-enhancing and depression-decreasing neurotransmitters like dopamine and serotonin.[7]

Newberg and Waldman remind us that anxious individuals have a more difficult time suppressing negative thoughts and often get caught up in the repetitive process of rumination. This, unfortunately, strengthens the neural circuits that generate anxiety and embed the information into long-term memory banks. No bueno! So, take charge. Take those toxic thoughts captive by the power given to you by God and stand firm.

NOTES

[1]Leaf, *Switch on Your Brain*.

[2]Kelly McGonigal, "Your Brain on Meditation," *Mindful*, December 6, 2010. http://www.mindful.org/your-brain-on-meditation.

[3]Tom Ireland, "What Does Mindfulness Meditation Do to Your Brain?," *Scientific American,* June 12, 2014, http://blogs.scientificamerican.com/guest-blog/what-does-mindfulness-meditation-do-to-your-brain/.

[4]Brent Lambert, "Harvard Unveils MRI Study Proving Meditation Literally Rebuilds the Brain's Gray Matter in 8 Weeks," *FEELguide*, November 19, 2014, http://www.feelguide.com/2014/11/19/harvard-unveils-mri-study-proving-meditation-literally-rebuilds-the-brains-gray-matter-in-8-weeks/.

[5]Michele Rosenthal, "Train Your Brain: How to Reduce Anxiety through Mindfulness and Meditation," *Rewire Me*, February 15, 2014, https://www.rewireme.com/brain-insight/train-your-brain-how-to-reduce-anxiety-through-mindfulness-and-meditation/.

[6]Andrew Newberg and Mark Robert Waldman, *How God Changes Your Brain: Breakthrough Findings from a Leading Neuroscientist* (New York: Ballantine Books, 2009), Kindle.

[7]Newberg and Waldman, Kindle.

Chapter Twelve

EXPERIENCING GOD: WHAT GOD *REALLY* DOES TO YOUR BRAIN

You don't think your way into a new kind of living but live your way into a new kind of thinking.

—Henri Nouwen

Dr. Andrew Newberg has spent the last fifteen plus years at the University of Pennsylvania studying spirituality and its effects on the human brain. In his latest book with Mark Robert Waldman, they explain, "If you contemplate God long enough, something surprising happens in the brain. Neural functioning begins to change. Different circuits become activated, while others become deactivated."[1]

Newberg and Waldman also say that there are eight specific functions that lead to optimum mental health and well-being that not only will exercise your brain but will change its neurochemistry:

- Smiling (try this when you're upset)
- Staying intellectually active (brain games, anyone?)

- Consciously relaxing (developing awareness and learning to focus)
- Yawning (at least ten times without stopping)
- Meditating (long-term contemplation on God)
- Aerobic exercise (consistency is key)
- Dialogue with others (fellowship and community)
- Faith (different neural structures shape our beliefs about God)

You may have heard some of these suggestions already, and some may even seem silly to you. While diving into a lengthy explanation of each is beyond the scope of this book, I can assure you that research has empirically validated the benefits of each of these. All of the little things we do to create optimum brain health and well-being have a cumulative effect on our mood, as well as on our neurochemistry.

There is no question that faith, meditation, prayer, and many of the other practices included in the spiritual disciplines do something powerful to change our neuro-networks. These contemplative practices not only change us, but they give space for us to be more attuned and present for the other people in our world. They are the foundation for empathy.

Concept of God

What does research say about our "God circuits" in the brain? Does it matter if you really believe in Jesus, or will meditating on any old thing change your neurochemistry? The answers are complex, but studies show that while different religious activities have different effects on your brain, the key seems to be the actual "act" of meditation. According to Newberg and Waldman's research, you could take God out of the equation and still impact the brain's neurocircuitry. Other studies have shown that the same benefits could be derived from different forms of meditation and relaxation such as yoga, progressive muscle relaxation, and deep breathing.[2]

One thing is for certain, each form of ritual that goes along with spirituality can change how you think and feel about God. For Christian believers, I would add that what we feel or think about God has little to do with the truth. I may feel angry at God, alienated from God, or confused about God. I may even believe God doesn't care about me, but none of that is true. We have to base our thoughts and beliefs about God on scriptural truth. This doesn't mean we deny our thoughts and feelings; it just means we have to challenge them in light of God's Word.

All of us have developed a concept of God. We have ideas, images, feelings, beliefs about who God is. We looked at this idea when we talked earlier about attachment theory. Relationships with our parents or other key attachment figures shape how we do relationships. All of these relationship rules are encoded in our neurocircuitry and later serve as a lens from which we view relationship with God.

Each part of our brain is involved in creating, integrating, and giving emotional meaning to the concept of "God" we've developed. Right now you may be wondering, so what? Does all this really matter? Absolutely. It matters, because the goal of all these practices is transformation. The Bible says, "Do not be conformed to this world, but be transformed by the renewal of your mind" (Rom. 12:2 ESV). Real transformation—the kind the Bible describes—is only derived from a personal relationship with the living God. The spiritual disciplines are the gateway to this transformation. Again, Newberg and Waldman's words resonate:

> Intense, long-term contemplation of God and other
> spiritual values appears to permanently change the

structure of those parts of the brain that control
our moods, give rise to our conscious notions of
self, and shape our sensory perceptions of the world.
Contemplative practices strengthen a specific neurological circuit that generates peacefulness, social awareness,
and compassion for others. Spiritual practices also can
be used to enhance cognition, communication, and cre-
ativity, and over time can even change our neurological
perception of reality itself.[3]

Let's look at a couple other spiritual practices that are shown to
have powerful effects on the brain.

The Discipline of Worship

The Bible calls us to worship. Worship is our response to a loving
God who not only created us, but who sent his Son as an aton-
ing sacrifice for our sins. God is a seeker-God. He seeks us out
to restore us in right relationship with himself. Worship is our
expression of love back to God for all he has done for us. Here are
a few verses to consider about worship:

The true worshipers will worship the Father in spirit and
truth, for the Father is seeking such people to worship
him. (John 4:23 ESV)

Through Jesus, therefore, let us continually offer to God
a sacrifice of praise—the fruit of lips that openly profess
his name. (Heb. 13:15)

I will bless the LORD at all times: his praise shall
continually be in my mouth. (Ps. 34:1 KJV)

My mouth is filled with your praise, declaring your
splendor all day long. . . . I will praise you more and
more. (Ps. 71:8, 14)

We are to give God the glory due his name through the sacrifice of praise and worship. *Okay*, you might be thinking, *what does any of this have to do with changing my brain? How can worshiping and praising God really do anything to my brain?* Let's take a look.

It's easy for us to thank God when things are going well, but it takes a lot more intention and deliberate effort to praise him when life sucks. When things are difficult in life, when we're experiencing loss, sorrow, trials, and temptations, where do our thoughts take us? Right to the negative, self-defeating thinking we've been talking about all through this book. When we praise and worship God, we are shifting our awareness from toxic thoughts and forcing our minds to focus on God. If we can hold our attention there, several things happen: relaxation, deeper awareness, and attentiveness—all things that help in the rewiring process.

Consider this: let's say you're reading this book, and you're pretty focused on it. You probably haven't paid too much attention to the process of reading, but if something happens—say your child runs by and accidently drops something heavy on your foot—your attention now is shifted to your foot because it's throbbing. You won't have any problem focusing on your foot. You will be keyed in to the sensations of pain you're experiencing, the red color on your foot from the blow, if your foot feels warm or cold, if the accident cut your skin and you're bleeding. All of this will be in your conscious awareness.

Now, try switching your focus back to the book. Really *notice* the book because I've mentioned it. Now you may become aware of all kinds of things about reading the book that weren't in your conscious awareness before. How light or heavy does it feel? Is the cover smooth or rough? What do the printed images on the cover say to you? Is the type large or small? Is it colorful? How does it feel in your hands as you hold it? What sensations do you notice?

In all the exercises we've practiced so far, I've instructed you to consistently bring your mind back to center when it wanders, or back to your breath, then back to whatever you were practicing. When you practice shifting your awareness, it intensifies the experience. Try this: bring your focus to the book cover, now the pages, now the ink on the pages, now the type, now the texture. Now shift again and notice your foot. Focus on it. Now shift your focus to the breath. Stay there. Deep inhale. Pause. Deep exhale. All of this is enlarging your conscious experience, and it's strengthening key circuitry in your brain.

When I was feeling overwhelmed about my loss, the last thing I wanted to do was worship or praise God. At first I was angry that he had allowed something so horrible to happen. After I worked through all that, there were some days I was so upset and distraught I just plain ol' didn't want to. But doing it anyway did a couple of things for me. First, as I started to praise God, I noticed that I became more relaxed. Second, I was able to observe my thoughts and feelings flowing through my mind, but I wasn't focused on making any judgments about them. In other words, I learned just to observe them from a distance.

Now I've learned that if anxious toxic thoughts come into my mind about Mike or the trauma, I don't dismiss them. I notice them. Then I shift my awareness back to my praise, or to my breath, or to whatever else I may be doing. What this does is increase frontal lobe consciousness that serves to calm the emotional circuits in the brain. This means anxiety dissipates and depression can lift.

The Act of Worship

So now let's apply some of this to the discipline of worship and to how it can change your neurocircuitry. While this isn't a book on praise and worship, a couple of things may help to set the stage for you as you begin to practice the discipline of worship. First, the idea of worship is to experience the holy presence of God. That's why cultivating the disciplines of silence and solitude will have tremendous benefits because they will set the stage for an inner attitude of the heart, as well as calming your spirit before you enter into worship.

Worship invites us to enter into the presence of God. This requires stillness. In Psalm 46:10, the Lord says, "Be still, and know that I am God." Developing a life where we are cultivating an inner silence and a listening ear to our heavenly Father will not only calm us but will teach us to focus. When we have an attitude or a mindset of worship, we are continually in communication with God.

Often, when we think of worship, we think of a corporate setting on Sunday mornings, but worship can be done anytime, anywhere because it is really an attitude of the heart. So start by learning to talk to God. Practice his presence each day in quiet reflection. Pray continually. Be aware of cultivating an attitude of gratefulness and thanksgiving.

Research by gratitude expert Robert Emmons shows that practicing gratitude daily is highly beneficial to physical health, to psychological well-being, and in relationships with others. Emmons found that "gratitude blocks toxic, negative emotions, such as envy, resentment, regret—emotions that can destroy our happiness. There's even recent evidence . . . showing that gratitude can reduce the frequency and duration of episodes of depression."[4] Here's what studies have shown:

- "A 2009 series of studies using MRIs of brains showed that the limbic system in general—of which the hypothalamus is a part—is activated whenever we feel gratitude, pride, or do something altruistic for somebody else."[5]

- "Basically, a brain that is experiencing gratitude, specifically gratitude focused on a specific person . . . is flooded with positive chemicals of a unique kind."[6]
- A team at the University of Southern California "found that grateful brains showed enhanced activity in two primary regions: the anterior cingulate cortex (ACC) and the medial prefrontal cortex (mPFC). These areas have been previously associated with emotional processing, interpersonal bonding and rewarding social interactions, moral judgment, and the ability to understand the mental states of others."[7]

Worshiping God is practicing gratitude, and that's another sure-fire way to rewire your brain!

The Discipline of Prayer

The Bible tells us to "pray without ceasing" or "pray continually." "Rejoice always," 1 Thessalonians 5:16–18 tells us. "Pray continually, give thanks in all circumstances; for this is God's will for you in Christ Jesus." Why should we do this? Because we're commanded to. Does it help? Absolutely. Newberg and Waldman's research says this about how prayer changes our brain:

> Brief prayer . . . has not yet been shown to have a direct effect upon cognition, and it even appears to increase depression in older individuals who are not religiously affiliated. However, when prayer is incorporated into longer forms of intense meditation, or practiced within the context of weekly religious activity, many health benefits have been found, including greater length of life.[8]

Newberg and Waldman go on to say, "Prayer is generally conducted for only a few minutes at a time, and we believe that it is the intense, ongoing focus on a specific object, goal, or idea that stimulates the cognitive circuits in the brain."[9]

Dr. Leaf weighs in on the power of prayer saying,

> It has been found that 12 minutes of daily focused prayer over an 8-week period can change the brain to such an extent that it can be measured on a brain scan. This type of prayer increases activity in brain areas associated with social interaction compassion and sensitivity to others. It also increases frontal lobe activity as focus and intentionality increase.

She also explains that "There are over twelve hundred studies linking intentional prayer and overall health and longevity. Meta-analyses in various medical journals have compiled results that show that intentional prayer significantly affects healing."[10]

What actually happens when we pray? Pretty much the same thing that happens when we meditate. When your mind is directed to relaxation and rest such as in meditation, worship, and prayer, there is a lot of activity between the networks of your brain and your mind. In these restful states, the brain actually moves into a reflective, self-directed state, and the more we practice those states, the more we carve out new neuropathways that connect us to God.

The Discipline of Solitude

Nobody likes this one, least of all me! It's not that I don't like being alone. I do. It's just that being alone reminds me of a deeper kind of aloneness that I don't want to face: being alone with myself. That kind of emptiness drills down deep. Perhaps we're afraid of what we'll find. We feel insecure in who we are. We're afraid we don't have what it takes to cut it in life. We're afraid God won't show up for us.

When I lost Mike, I believed that I had lost all security. He was everything to me, and for me. That's a dangerous place to live. I still struggle with this, but in my heart, I know my only security rests in Christ. That will never change, no matter what I lose—and trust me, one day everything we hold dear will slip through our fingers. All that will remain is him. All this being said, though, solitude has afforded me the most personal way to connect with God and to come face to face with my own inadequacy. That, in turn, has led me to the inexhaustible sufficiency of Christ.

As I've mentioned, the discipline of silence goes hand in hand with solitude. We generally don't like either of these disciplines because they make us feel helpless, but there is no better way to foster inner focus and transformation (as well as brain transformation). There is no soil more fertile than that which solitude and silence afford us. There is no better way to practice all the techniques you have learned in this book than to be still and alone.

How can we enter into solitude? By taking small steps. I did a quiet retreat in a beautiful setting in Maryland a year after Mike died. If you can, plan these getaways several times a year. You will be amazed how recharged you will feel. If you can't do that, try carving out some early morning time where you simply lie in bed and think, pray, and reflect on God. Breathe. Take advantage of little moments when you can be alone and still. The uncomfortableness that stillness may initially create will eventually give way to calm. You will begin to relish the chance to get quiet and alone because of the benefits you will reap. Don't give up on this practice. It can be life-changing.

Pressing On

The truth is that life is hard. For some, life can be brutal. As I finish this book, three years have passed since the trauma. I am still in process. There was no magic wand to be waved. No simple words that were spoken. No easy way out from this unthinkable loss. It was the hardest work I have ever done and struggle to keep on doing in order to make it home. Thoughts, memories, visions, feelings, people, places, and things can all bring up very vivid good, and not-so-good, recollections for me—and for you. All of this can give way to toxic thinking. Now, you have some key truths and some powerful tools to help you not only stay in the battle but win the war!

The truths written in this book, as well as all the empirically validated research from all the other excellent writings I've cited here, will work. The question is, will *you* work them? If I can leave you, my reader, with a couple of lasting thoughts, they are these: what you think about and what you set your mind on are what you will experience more day after day. Only *you* hold the power, with God's help, to choose to change your life, retrain your brain, and decide on your behavior. My prayer is that you will consistently practice the skills you've learned here and reap the benefits of change they will afford you. May God be with you on your journey.

NOTES

[1] Newberg and Waldman, Kindle.

[2] Newberg and Waldman, Kindle.

[3] Newberg and Waldman, Kindle.

[4] Robert Emmons, "Why Gratitude Is Good," *Greater Good Magazine,* November 16, 2010, https://greatergood.berkeley.edu/article/item/why _gratitude_is_good/.

[5] J. R. Thorpe, "6 Ways Gratitude Affects Your Brain," *Bustle,* November 13, 2015, https://www.bustle.com/articles/123590-6-ways-gratitude-affects-your -brain.

[6] Thorpe.

[7] Adam Hoffman, "What Does a Grateful Brain Look Like?" *Greater Good Magazine,* November 16, 2015, https://greatergood.berkeley.edu/article/item /what_does_a_grateful_brain_look_like.

[8]Newberg and Waldman, Kindle.
[9]Newberg and Waldman, Kindle.
[10]Leaf, *Switch on Your Brain*.

"This is a rare book of encouragement and hope that takes on some of life's most difficult questions. With honesty and wisdom, Rita goes beyond trite theory or psychologizing on how to merely survive losses to specific ways that, with God's help, we can actually thrive, grow, deepen, and mature in the midst of the inevitable pain, agony, discouragement, and despair that comes with the losses in our lives."

—GARY J. OLIVER, ThM, PhD, Executive Director of the Center for Healthy Relationships, Professor of Psychology and Practical Theology, John Brown University

SHATTERED

FINDING HOPE AND HEALING THROUGH THE LOSSES OF LIFE

by **Rita A. Schulte**

Shattered explores how unidentified or unresolved loss impacts every area of life, especially your relationship with God. The long-range impact of these losses is often obscured, buried beneath the conscious surface in an attempt to avoid pain. In this book, Rita calls you to notice the losses of life and fight the battle to reclaim and reinvest your heart after loss with faith-based strategies.

$14.99

LEAFWOOD
PUBLISHERS
an imprint of Abilene Christian University Press

www.leafwoodpublishers.com | 877-816-4455 (toll free)